LIFE 101

Money Management and Adulting Made Simple

LIFE 101

Money Management and Adulting Made Simple

Marlene Jenkins Cooper

Songs of Judah Publishing

Philadelphia, PA

Life 101: Money Management and Adulting Made Simple / Marlene Jenkins Cooper

The information in this book is for your general knowledge and is not a substitute for professional financial or legal advice.

Book Layout ©2017 BookDesignTemplates.com

ISBN: 978-0-9961227-0-2

1. Financial Literacy 2. Adulting 3. Money Management 4. Budgeting 5. Self Help

First Edition

Printed in United States of America

Table of Contents

Dedication

To all of my former students
who lived, breathed, and experienced
"Life 101"
in the classroom

"By failing to prepare, you are preparing to fail."

— Benjamin Franklin

Foreword

Life is a never-ending series of learning opportunities. As long as we embrace failure and continue to grow, success is inevitable. There can be a lot of fear about the idea of growing up—maybe you are moving out of your parent's home, perhaps you are starting at college or starting vocational training, you might be taking some time off from school to just figure out what you really want to do, or already working a full-time job. Either way, the endless possibilities and responsibilities lurking around the corner can be daunting. Adulting is challenging, but with open-mindedness and planning, the possibilities are as wide as your imagination.

I had the privilege of taking Ms. Cooper's *Life 101* class as a seventh-grade student. My first memory of that class was looking at my given annual salary and thinking, "What can I do to make sure I can afford to buy a terracotta 2008 Ford Edge?" The assignment was to use Microsoft Excel to create a monthly budget for all necessities—rent, food, utilities, transportation, student loans, socializing, miscellaneous— and all I knew was that I needed to do whatever I could to afford this car. With a yearly salary of about $25,000, I managed to rent a very small room in a house and stay up to date with all utilities (those rates were set by Ms. Cooper according to 2008 prices), afford transportation to and from work, and buy the car! What suffered in this scenario was my budget for food, social life, and miscellaneous needs. Based on the budget I had set up, I was hungry, lonely, and couldn't afford a doctor's appointment if an emergency occurred. But I had my car!

Looking back, it was quite silly of me to plan my financial life around a car. However, the skills that I learned in that class, particularly that budgeting assignment, have proven useful in my adult life. Because I was exposed to adult tasks such as searching for an apartment, researching post-secondary education programs, managing student loan debt and credit, and saving for vacation at such an early age, those tasks now feel a little less daunting. They are still challenging sometimes, but I have the knowledge of *Life 101* and my lived experience to support me.

Perhaps one of the most important lessons I learned from Ms. Cooper was that asking questions and asking for help doesn't mean you are any less smart or capable than those who don't. Ms. Cooper is one of the most generous and passionate educators I've had the pleasure of meeting. She is a life-long learner and is always willing to share her knowledge with young people. The future I imagined for myself in seventh grade has only continued to expand, and because of Ms. Cooper's teaching, I am able to plan for my dreams to come true. Preparedness makes adulting manageable.

Manna-Symone Middlebrooks
MFA Directing Candidate, Northwestern University 2023

Acknowledgements

First and foremost, I would like to thank God for giving me the inspiration and opportunity to write *Life 101: Money Management and Adulting Made Simple*. I would also like to express my gratitude to the many people, including former students, family, and friends, who provided support with their opinions and thoughts for this book.

I am grateful to my former principals, Chris Sadjian-Peacock and Sonia Rodrigues Perez, who believed in and allowed me to teach the *Life 101* curriculum to our students. Many thanks, as well, to the parents of my students for their support and for sharing with their children to help them with their real-life assignments. Thanks to my former students who lived, breathed, experienced, and completed the exercises for *"Life 101."* It was my pleasure to teach the *Life 101* course to you and prepare you for today, adulting.

Marlene Jenkins Cooper

Part I

What's Life All About?

CHAPTER 1

Introduction to Adulting

Adulting is taking on the responsibilities and activities of adulthood. Sometimes while on the journey of life, the following major life stages after graduating high school may occur in a different order in one's life than below. Because of circumstances and personal choices, not everyone will have the same life experience nor experience each of the stages. Nevertheless, this book will plan for each stage of life.

Life Stages

For the practical purposes of this book, the following steps will be identified as:

I. After the College Graduation/My New Career
II. The Single Life
III. The Married Life
IV. Married with Children
V. Possible Life Changes With the "D's"
VI. Retirement

Setting Goals

A goal is something one wants to strive to achieve. It is important to have goals and ambitions for each step of your life. Identify the goals you want to complete, reach, or strive for in your life. Each day of your life should be productive. Daily goals will keep productive people on track to meet them. Wasted time is never refunded, and once a moment in time is gone, it is gone forever.

Where do you see yourself in five, ten, or fifteen years? Let's think about it. Create a plan and write it down! A written plan is a work in progress. Stay focused on meeting the goals and develop steps to achieving them.

First, you should set goals, then establish strategies to accomplish those goals, and finally set a timeframe for completion. Devise a plan on how to accomplish each goal. For example, it is impossible to have a goal to travel to two different countries next year without having a valid passport or completing an application for one.

"A goal without a plan is just a wish" is a famous quote by the 20th-century French author Antoine de Saint-Exupery.[1] Now is the time to plan for the experiences that will occur down the road called life's journey. This is not to say that life experiences

---

[1] "A Goal without a Plan is Just a Wish: 3 Lessons for This Quote", n.d. Accessed September 8, 2020. https://www.developgoodhabits.com/goal-without-plan/

will happen as we have planned, but at least a plan is in motion. "If we fail to plan, the plan will fail." Sometimes, we may fail to meet our expectations, but we must continue to reach for the stars. We fall down, but we can get up again. Sometimes there may be challenges to meeting your goals. Unfortunately, some goals are never met. Keep trying; never give up.

In every life step of life, there is a set of goals you should strive to meet. Your short- and long-time goals should be written and reviewed at least twice a month. Try hard to achieve these goals. Choose financial, educational, physical, interest, career, relationship (friendship), and spiritual goals. Goals should be written in a journal, printed on paper, and/or posted somewhere.

A vision board is another means of viewing your goals, dreams, ambitions, and aspirations. A vision board can be made of paper, poster board, foam, or cardboard, with pictures pasted on the board depicting your goals, dreams, and aspirations with descriptive words about the vision. Revisit these goals at least twice a month, if not more.

Strive each day to fulfill your short- and long-term goals. Re-evaluate your goals every three months (every quarter) or when the need arises. Unfortunately, it is possible that you will not meet your goals by the appointed time, but still continue trying to meet them. Remember, as the saying goes, "Rome was not built in one day." When the goal is completed, it can be crossed off the list, and the date of completion written next to the goal. Congratulations! Job well done.

Many people post their goals and others make a vision board with their goals displayed via pictures from magazines or photographs and/or effective descriptive words. Post your goals on your private bathroom mirror, near the light switch in your bedroom, on the refrigerator, or on another visual spot that is often seen by you.

Be mindful of the people who will read and view your plan. Goals do not have to be posted for all to see. If posted, relatives, friends, and other viewers may give positive or negative opinions and/or may remind you of your goals and offer their opinions. Others may remind you of your unmet goals, and some may help you achieve them. Work your goals into your everyday life. To get a full perspective, listen to their comments about your goals and aspirations, but remember that you make the final decision on what comments are for consideration. Reach for your goals and commit to making them happen!

Short-Term and Long-Term Goals

Your life should have goals included. There should be a set of realistic achievable short-term and long-term goals. At each stage of your adult life, your goals will change. Stay focused on meeting goals and develop steps to reach them. A plan is necessary to fulfill and meet all goals.

Short-term goals are goals that can be attained in one to five years. Always have goals that can be attainable in a certain (specific) amount of time. Goals are not always met in the time allotted, but strive to make it happen with a plan.

Long-term goals are goals that can be attained within a longer time period. These goals are a long reach and need many years to complete. In your long-term goals, take baby steps towards completion.

Consider using the S.M.A.R.T. goal method for achieving success with your goals. The acronym S.M.A.R.T. stands for Specific, Measurable, Achievable, Relevant, and Time-bound. Use these criteria to assist with attaining your goals.[2]

Another tool for meeting your goals is repeating a mantra to yourself daily. A mantra is a statement or saying that is repeated to yourself every morning to keep your focus intact. For example, "I desire to make great food choices to be fit and healthy." This is a great mantra, but how? Create a food plan for a healthy lifestyle. When? Immediately!

My Goals

If you aim for nothing, you will surely hit it. Plan to achieve! What do you want to achieve in the next five or six years? These

---

[2] SMART Goal-Definition, Guide, and Importance of Goal Setting", n.d., accessed September 7, 2020, · https://coroporatefinanceinstitiute.com/resources/knowledge/other/smart-goal/.

goals need to be written down, realistic, time frame set, and measurable.

Sample Short-Term Goals
(1-4-year Plan)

1. Purchase a new car
2. Read five novels for pleasure and two nonfiction books
3. Save $5,000.00 or more in a savings account
4. Learn a new hobby (i.e., sewing, painting, archery, scrapbooking)

Sample Long-Term Goals
(5-10-year plan)

1. Purchase a home
2. Travel to one to three different countries
3. Save $10,000.00 or more in a savings account
4. Learn a musical instrument.
5. Earn an educational degree or get an additional degree.

My Goals
Exercise #1: Short-Term Goals (1-5-year Plan)

Date: _____

1. _____

2. _____

3. _____

4. _____

5. _____

Long Term Goals (5-10-year Plan)

1. _____

2. _____

3. _____

4. _____

5. _____

Adulthood is here, and you are responsible for every aspect of your life. Making day-to-day decisions concerning life experiences, health, and finances is the adulting way. Hopefully, prior to adulthood, you have watched your parents, teachers, family members, mentors, and older friends "do life." There are computer and phone applications (apps) to assist you with every aspect of adulting and tracking your goals. You may know what you want and do not want for your life, but it is permissible to ask questions of others and research your questions or concerns on adulting. A day without adulting does not exist. Adults are responsible for their own welfare. Permission to temporarily stop adulting for a moment is not granted.

As you read this book, underline important facts that speak to you and continue to research major facets about life experiences. Remember, you are not alone! Your peers are trying to figure out how to do "life" as well.

CHAPTER 2

Choosing Your Life's Path

After high school, what's next? Who declares that you are an adult—your high school principal, parents, or someone else? The United States government declares a person of legal age and an adult at eighteen years of age.

From elementary to high school, your teachers have been preparing students for this adulting moment. Hopefully, parents have also been preparing their children to spread their wings and fly after graduating from high school. Eighteen years of life should be enough time for a child to learn to make decisions based on their parent's teachings and directions. When will mommy and daddy kick their child out of the nest? Did you know that in nature, mother animals tell their young goodbye at specific times? After some nurturing and lessons, these animals learn how to survive on their own. Many mama birds push their young babies out of the nest to let them fly on their own.

Unfortunately, everyone is not ready or mature enough to begin adulting the day after high school or college graduation. Since we cannot stop the clock of life, hold back time, cancel, or delay the entire school's graduation for you, adulting must begin. So here comes life. Life cannot wait for you to be ready. Get ready! Here comes life!

In life, you must prepare for each upcoming stage of development. After graduating from high school and college, life begins anew. Be prepared, be ready, and take action. Decisions, decisions, and more decisions must be made. What path will you take? Will it be college or a vocational school or one of the armed forces, or will your path lead directly into the workforce? The answer to these questions must be made in advance of your high school graduation and not on the day after. Choose your life's pathway and how you will make a living to support yourself. One must prepare for life after high school or college.

If you want to join one of the armed forces, which armed forces will meet your needs? The military includes The Navy, Marine Corps, Air Force, Coast Guard, and The Army. These armed forces are under the Department of Defense of the United States. After serving in the military, you might be interested to know that the GI bill is an educational benefit to help veterans who qualify attend college.

If a college education or the armed forces is not in the future, enter the workforce and get a job. Where do you want to work and what jobs are you qualified to work? What skills do you have? Can you type, program computers, manage people, or do you possess other skills? Sixty-five percent of all job openings in the United States will need a post-secondary education in 2020, as stated in the executive summary report entitled "Recovery: Job Growth and Education Requirements through 2020," by Georgetown University. This report further states that "thirty-five percent of all job openings will require at least a bachelor's degree."[3]

To help with the above questions, ask your parents, college school counselor, mentor, community worker, or relatives for advice. Ask questions! As a young adult, listen and take the advice given by parents/guardians. It is your option to take their advice or leave it.

The World Wide Web gives a wealth of knowledge to your quest for answers. Finally, there are a gazillion books on the market to read to help on your adult journey.

Let's start the journey! Remember, life is a process. In four or five years, where will you be?

---

[3] "Recovery: Job Growth And Education Requirements Through 2020 ...", n.d. Accessed September 7, 2020. https://cew.georgetown.edu/cew-reports/recovery-job-growth-and-education-requirements-through-2020/.

The Choice

How many times have you been asked, "What do you want to be when you grow up?" Although you may change your mind several times between now and when you find that ultimate career, there must be a starting point.

What skills and education do I need to fulfill my aspirations, dreams, and goals? Do I need college, vocational school, or on-the-job training? Going to college is one way for you to experience life and develop responsibility while learning about a specific course of study.

What is the difference between a career and a job? A career is a profession that one has studied, prepared for, and seeks to advance through experiences. In my estimation, a job is a place where the one main objective is to make money and earn a paycheck! Unfortunately, it is possible to have a career turn into a job because of unhappiness in the workplace. When this happens, begin to look for a new place of employment or change careers.

When looking for a career, the salary should not be your ultimate goal, but rather the love of the occupation. The salary is very important, but it should not drive your decision on a career choice. Choose a career that is aligned with your passion—one that is fulfilling and self-rewarding. A career should be one that you would work for free if need be. (I am not advocating working for free!) Nonetheless, the career has to be able to fully support your lifestyle.

One cannot and should not work at a career just for the money it brings. The career must be your passion! Chase your passion, not the dollar. However, your career choice must be able to financially support your lifestyle. Once again, what do you want to do when you grow up? If there is not an answer at this present time, research, explore the possibilities, and ask questions on your quest to find the answer.

Since the age of five, I knew that I wanted to be a teacher. However, my students often told me, "Ms. Cooper, it doesn't take all that to teach this subject." My effervescence and passion for bequeathing knowledge at 8:25 AM is too much for some.

If you are late to the process, all is not lost. It is time to play "catch up". If you have not identified your future goals up to this point, you still can plan and begin to pursue your aspirations.

One's educational level of attainment affects one's earning power. In 2019, the US government posted statistics on the earnings according to the level of education.

Educational Attainment	Median usual weekly earnings
Doctoral degree	$1,883.00
Professional degree	$1,861.00
Master's degree	$1,497.00

Bachelor's degree	$1,248.00
Associate's degree	$887.00
Some college, no degree	$833.00
Less than a high school diploma	$592.00[4]

Usually, the more education you acquire, the more money you get. Do not feel discouraged if you are a late bloomer. However, now is the time to get started on the process of figuring out and researching what you want to do in the next step of your life. Now is the time. Get started.

Four years later...

Your college graduation is now over. You have moved out of the dorm or your student apartment. Now it is time to get a job and be self-sufficient. Being self-sufficient means taking care of yourself without financial help from parents, guardians, or relatives.

Maybe your four years of military service is complete and are honorably discharged. It is time to do life on your own.

At 22 years of age, many graduates are single when they graduate from undergraduate studies. However, some people are

---

[4] "Unemployment Rates and Earnings by Educational Attainment: U.S. ...", n.d. Accessed September 7, 2020. https://www.bls.gov/emp/chart-unemployment-earnings-education.htm

single with a child(ren) or married. Use the information that pertains to your status.

Your undergraduate college graduation is now over. Before graduation, look for a full-time job to support yourself. Be self-reliant and self-dependent.

Steps to Looking for a Job

The Resume

A resume is a document that informs a potential employer of your personal information, education, qualifications, and job experience, and previous jobs to qualify for a position at a company or organization. Most people want a great high paying or an adequate steady paying job or career. Before this happens, companies use resumes to determine if potential employees meet the qualifications and are good fits for the company. There is a department at most businesses, companies, and organizations called the Human Resource (HR) department, which is responsible for employees and their benefits. The HR department often interviews, receives resumes, hires, handles labor relations, and administers staff development on topics that concerns their department.

Post resumes on online job-seeking sites. Look for jobs at your present or former college's resource center, company websites, internet job seeking sites, and job fairs. You can also seek opportunities to intern for companies or organizations. Network with persons in your field, contact family, friends, club, sorority, and fraternity members who may have job leads.

Fill out job applications. Most job applications and opportunities to post your resume are now online. Complete all the necessary information correctly and honestly.

To make things easier, use a template to help you complete your resume. A resume template is a ready-made resume, which allows you to input your information in the designated slots. There are online wizards to help you create a resume also. I recommend that you have someone review your resume before sending and/or posting it.

Resumes should be one page with Times New Roman font style and font size 12. Other fonts, such as Calibri, Garamond, Georgia, and Helvetica, are acceptable. However, only use one of the fonts above.

List schooling and experience from most recent to least recent. Sometimes the most recent and job-related information impresses the reviewer. Be truthful and honest. If references are required, first contact those persons and ask permission before listing them and their contact information on your resume. Have someone review and critique your resume before sending it out. Spell check and consider using a resume template. There is a plethora of sample online resumes in your field along with resume generators.

Exercise #2: The Resume

Complete the necessary items below.

Name- _____

Address - _____

Phone- _____ Email - _____

EDUCATION –
(List current or most recent first and then in reverse chronological order.)

_____

_____

_____

_____

ACTIVITIES

_____

_____

_____

SKILLS

_____

_____

_____

Jane Doe
Human Resource Specialist

555 Market Street Somewhere, NY 19005
(555) 555-5550 ● janedoe@gmail.com

Education

Cooper State University; Nowhere, PA, Bachelor of Arts, Business Administration, 2014 ● GPA: 3.95; Dean's List 2013, 2014

Experience

Jenkins Graphic Designs; Somewhere, NY, 19005 September 2014-2018

Human Resource Specialist

- Implement HR polices
- Facilitate workshops on health benefits
- Interview and hire capable persons
- Engage in conflict resolution

Activities

President – Human Resources Management of New York -2016
Choir President – Cooper University Choir - 2014
Senior Class President - Cooper State University Student Government, Nowhere, PA
Member, Cooper State University Volleyball Team 2011- 2014

Skills Profile

Proficient in Microsoft Word, Excel, & PowerPoint, and Adobe Photoshop

The Job Search

Ask job recruiters, check job hunting websites, attend job and career fairs, visit your college's job placement office, and ask for tips on possible job openings from family, friends, and acquaintances. Look for people who are working in the field and ask them for assistance in acquiring a job.

If you hear, "Sorry, the position has been filled by someone else," remember that rejection is not denial forever. Face every rejection as a new opportunity to look for the right position. Keep looking! Do not give up.

Interviews

There are many types of interviews. The two basic types are phone and in-person interviews. Preliminary interviews are sometimes administered on the phone. A phone interview allows the interviewer to ask opening questions and eliminate those candidates that would not be a good fit for the company before an in-person interview is scheduled. For those that live far away, a phone interview is sometimes used as a primary option. A personal interview is a face-to-face meeting with the interviewer.

Dress for Success

Have you ever heard the term "dress for success"? Employers often judge the applicant by what he or she wears to the interview, as well as by what the applicant has worn in pictures on social media. Be mindful of the personal pictures you post on social media. Current and future employers read the internet posts of potential employees. When going to an in-person interview, dress as if you are going to a job and not to the club or sporting event. Do a web search for pictures of professional adults in dress for success attire to get ideas for outfits.

Ladies	**Men**
Dress	Suit and tie
Skirt, Blazer, & blouse	Sports jacket, dress pants,
Pantsuit	and dress shirt
Dress pants and blouse	

Never wear the following items to an interview:

Midriff tops	Flip-flops
T-shirts	Jeans with holes or rips
Jeans	Sneakers
Stilettos	Shorts
Mini (very short) skirt	

Recommendations

Many companies want recommendations from others about you and your work ethic. However, some employers want specific recommendations from certain people, i.e., past employers, supervisors, and teachers. You always want positive recommendations. Never burn a bridge with former employers and supervisors! Keep communications open with all people. One never knows when a recommendation from someone specific to your job qualifications is needed. Before putting someone's name as a recommendation on a resume or application, always ask for their permission to list their name and contact information. Many companies follow up by contacting the people listed in the recommendation section of the resume.

The New Job

Congratulations!! You have acquired a new job. Your resume met the job qualifications, and the phone and/or personal interviews met their expectations. Before signing on the dotted line, have someone knowledgeable about job offers in your family or community read and review the letter. Listen to their advice and select the right options for you before making the health benefits choices and financial decisions with the HR department.

10 Tips for your New Employment

1. *Dress for Success; adhere to the dress code of your employer/company.*
2. *Arrive to work on time and leave at the designated time and not one minute before. Work the entirety of your contracted hours.*
3. *Give your employer your best during the entire time you are expected to work.*

23

4. *Speak the King's English with proper grammar and no profanity.*
5. *Use your cell phone only during breaks and lunchtime.*
6. *Be kind and considerate to your co-workers, custodial staff, cafeteria workers, and administrators. Be kind to everyone even if they do not return the kindness.*
7. *Remain professional at all times.*
8. *Keep your business's business to yourself. Insider information should not be spread around.*
9. *Answer the telephone with "Good morning". This is Jane Doe. How can I help you?"*
10. *Know who the CEO is and what they look like. Gather information on them and read various articles or books they have written.*

Income

Working a job results in earning wages. Wages are the monetary payment for hours worked. A paycheck contains the monetary funds that an employee earned. There are two ways to view income: gross and net income. Gross income is the total amount of money earned in a given pay period <u>before </u>any is deducted. Net income is the total amount of money earned in a given pay period <u>after</u> deductions.

Deductions

The municipality (city/town), state, and federal government of the employee are the first groups to receive monetary deductions

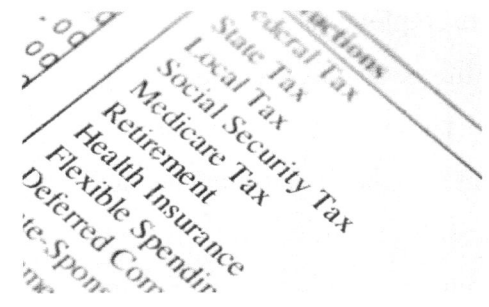

Figure 1-©Stephanie Frey/Adobe stock

from the paycheck before disbursement. Each group takes money out of the check to manage/run their jurisdiction. Remember the game of "Monopoly?" When a person lands on someone else's property, a tax is levied.

Taxes

Taxes are revenue collected by the city, state, and federal governments to operate in their jurisdiction. Therefore, each government may tax individuals who live, work, and own properties in their jurisdiction. Taxes are mandatory. These funds often pay for the salaries of government officials, trash and garbage removal, educational needs, teacher salaries and expenses of K-12 and higher education, health initiatives, road and highway construction and maintenance, police and fireman salaries, city/state/federal buildings, equipment, and the list goes on. "Uncle Sam", the affectionate name given to The United States government, wants his money upfront, and he receives it before the employer disperses the paycheck to the employee.

The employer notates the amount sent on the employee's behalf to the governmental agencies on the paycheck stub.

There are special and specific instances where taxes must be sent into the government agencies, i.e., the self-employed. In these cases, the federal, city, and state governments will often require quarterly taxes to be submitted throughout the year. A good rule of them for self-employed people and others is to estimate their taxes based on last year's earnings. Some government agencies even want the taxes sent in monthly. The government will receive the money due to them in due time! Ben Franklin is attributed as saying that there are two certainties in life: death and taxes.

The level of education you have attained often determines your salary range, albeit with some exceptions. More often than not, the more education one has, the more income he or she makes. A high school diploma employee generally makes much lower than someone employed with a college degree. Apprenticeships, learning a trade, and on-the-job training will offer higher incomes as well. Education is key!

In a perfect world, your income should meet all of one's needs and wants to maintain the lifestyle you desire. In his March 1958 "Advice for Living" column in Ebony Magazine, Martin Luther King stated in that too often [people] buy for their wants and beg for their needs.[5] A particular profession should not be chosen according to the salary it generates. You should love the work, people, and the responsibilities of your profession. If this is not the case, the income should at least meet your needs and maybe some of your wants. And sadly, if the income does not meet all of your needs, you must find ways to supplement the income with a part-time job, acquire a higher paying job, or lower your expenses. Salaried employees regularly receive a pre-determined amount of compensation each pay period on a weekly or less-frequent basis.[6] A wage is an amount one will be paid hourly multiplied by the hours worked.

Money

Money, or currency, is a financial unit of measurement for exchange. Currency has a different name, code, and symbol in each country. In the United States of America, the currency is called the US dollar, the currency code is USD and the currency symbol is $. Money is used to purchase items and pay for

---

[5] "'Advice for Living' | The Martin Luther King, Jr., Research and ...", n.d. Accessed September 7, 2020. https://kinginstitute.stanford.edu/king-papers/documents/advice-living-6.

[6] "Fact Sheet #17G: Salary Basis Requirement and the Part 541 ...", n.d., accessed January 5, 2020, https://www.dol.gov/agencies/whd/fact-sheets/17g-overtime-salary.

services. Who wants to work for free when they need funds to support themselves and/or their families? Compensation for work completed is necessary for most people. (Volunteerism is necessary too, but money is needed to support basic needs.)

Money must be respected. If a purchase or bill of sale is made, there is an obligation and responsibility to pay the bill at the time the bill is due. If bills are not paid or paid when due, there are financial consequences. If possible, pay your bills as soon as possible, and do not wait until the due date. If you can, pay the bill when the statement arrives.

Many companies add additional fees for bills not paid when due. The United States government sometimes garnishes wages from people who stop paying their student loans without authorization. Businesses who are not paid for their services or purchases or late payments report this information to credit bureaus. (Refer to page 47 for information on credit bureaus.)

Sample Paycheck Stub

...nings Information	Current	
...mal Gross	4,389.30	
...uctions	0.00	
...itions	0.00	
...rtime	0.00	Year to Date
EARNINGS TOTAL	4,389.30	5,277.30
...-Taxable Gross	351.14	418.18
...able Gross	3,971.12	4,859.12

...atutory & Other Deductions	Current	Year to Date
...ieral Withholding	311.17	311.17
...litional Federal Withholding	0.00	*****
...ite Withholding	135.96	135.96
...litional State Withholding	0.00	*****
...5DI	0.00	55.06
...iicare	62.67	75.55
...iicare Buyout	0.00	0.00
...ite Disability Insurance	0.00	0.00
...RS	351.14	351.14
...RS	0.00	0.00
...rnate Retirement	0.00	
	67.04	0.00

Figure 2- ©Josh Randall/Shutterstock

28

Money Withheld from Gross Income

Uncle Sam and other governmental agencies want their money upfront, and they receive it directly from the employer. The amount deducted is listed on the paystub. As stated earlier, persons in business for themselves must send their n to the respective governments during specific designated times throughout the year.

When my son received his first paycheck, his first words to me were "Who is FICA?" FICA took my money. Below are mandatory withdrawals from an employee paycheck.

Taxes

Mandatory taxes – City, State, Federal (government) Taxes

FICA- Federal Insurance Contributions Act- Monies are withdrawn from the employee's paycheck for their Social Security account that will use when the employee is eligible. Social Security is a benefit to those who worked a job and paid into the Social Security fund.

Medicare Part A- These funds are sent to the employee's Medicare federal government account for use when the employee reaches 67 years of age for medical expenses and benefits. (65 years of age for persons born before 1987.) https://www.ssa.gov/planners/retire/retirechart.html

Investments

Investments are another vehicle of income. Investments are only considered income when the investments earn money. Risk is involved when investing in stocks, bonds, mutual funds, and annuities. The risk includes losses, gains, or investments that remain the same in value during an investment period. A return of investments (ROI) is income. Money should grow over time. Let your future begin to grow as a young adult. Your future begins now. Something related to investments is compound interest, which is interest calculated on the initial principal, including all of the accumulated interest from previous periods on a deposit or loan.[7] (More on investments later chapters.)

Diversification of stocks is one of the major keys to investing. Have different types of financial vehicles in your portfolio. The rule of the thumb is not to have the same type of investments in your portfolio. Mutual funds have a diverse portfolio of different stocks and bonds. Investing over a long time period is a key factor in winning! Investments must be monitored! Please consult a certified financial advisor for help with investment strategies and investments. Finally, beware of the get-rich-quick schemes.

---

[7] "Compound Interest Definition", n.d. Accessed September 7, 2020. https://www.investopedia.com/terms/c/compoundinterest.asp.

Additional Monies Withheld

These deductions are optional:

Union dues – Union members are required to pay for union membership and representation, and the money is usually withdrawn from the employee's paycheck.

Life Insurance – These funds are deducted for life insurance benefits.

Health Insurance – Based on the employee's benefits, these funds are deducted for health, dental, vision, and prescription benefits.

Savings – A specific amount set by the employee sent to their personal savings account at their financial institution.

401(K) or 403(B) – Annuity payments are sent to your annuity retirement savings account. Some employers match contributing funds up to a specific amount.

There are additional line items that each employer has, such as employee donations to charities. Many employers offer payroll deduction to charities of your choice. It is important to give to charities. Give of your time and monies to charities that have a non-profit status. Gifts to charities may be tax-deductible. Check with a tax professional.

Another mode of charitable giving is tithing. Tithing is giving ten percent of your income to your church or place of worship for the upkeep and support of the church. Consider volunteering your time to non-profit organizations and giving to non-profits, too. You must be generous with your time and money. If your hand is closed in a fist, additional money cannot enter, but if your hand is open, you can give and also receive.

With all the above deductions, the rest of the money is what you take home. This is why your net pay is called take-home pay. After all of the above is withdrawn from the gross paycheck, the remainder is what is left to live on. A planned working budget documents the expenses and income for the month. However, if living to paycheck to paycheck occurs each month, an additional part-time job or a higher paying job may be necessary.

Early in life, it is important to have and identify trustworthy professionals in your life. They are:

1. Medical personnel (primary care doctor, dentist, optometrist, gynecologist, cardiologist, etc.)
2. Auto mechanic
3. Attorney
4. Home repair specialist (Handyman, plumber, gardener, electrician, etc.)
5. Financial advisor or planner (Establish a good relationship with a qualified financial advisor or planner that will help grow your investments.)

Have a yearly physical, dental and vision checkups, and health screenings. Take care of your health. Use a knowledgeable auto mechanic that will handle all car repairs and inspections. For any legal matters, consult an attorney. For those who are homeowners, a home repair specialist is needed. Have his/her number on speed dial.

Although death is not a popular topic, our mortality is real. There is a need to have a plan for one's money, and a plan for your money, wealth, and belongings in case of death. When I taught this lesson to my students, I had to be very clear to them that life everlasting here on earth is not promised to anyone. School bus accidents happen quite often, car accidents occur every day, and children, adults, and animals die from illnesses. This is a sad reality.

While studying the comic opera *Gianni Schicchi* by Giacomo Puccini, my students learned about the music, the story, and about wills. The comic opera is about a family who wanted their dead uncle's will changed because he left all his millions and wealth to the church. The family hired a con artist named Gianni Schicchi, and he changed the will for them, but for a hefty price. Changing the will was of utmost importance to the greedy family. This is illegal, but in a hilarious way, the family was able to change the will.

As a class exercise, my *Life 101* and opera students were instructed to write their last will and testament. The students were surprised by the entire process and how specific they needed to be about what items and money would be left to which named individuals. Then, each student had to sign and date the document, along with a witness's signature.

As adults, a will is a legal document that provides information about one's wishes regarding money and belongings in case of death. Therefore, a last will and testament must be completed before one's death. Leaving your affairs in order in case of death is the responsible thing to do as an adult.

Although an attorney can assist in the matter of preparing a will, every state has different rules and regulations. In some states, a will can be written without an attorney. Check your state's regulations. Usually, if a will is not present at the time of death, the state will make the decisions for the distribution of the wealth to the deceased.

Part II

Money, Money, Money

CHAPTER 3

Let's Talk About Money

News break! Money does not grow on trees, but has to be earned. Now that you have a steady job with hopefully adequate income, how will you manage your money? Who does this money belong to? The money belongs to you, and it is your job to properly manage it. Your full name is written on the paycheck. Can you imagine if your employer decided to put your parents' names on your paycheck? This would upset you. The paycheck earnings are the result of your hard-earned work.

What does the paycheck look like? As an adult, you must be financially responsible and manage the income you earn. What will your income accomplish? Have you ever heard your grandmother or an older person say, "Do you know the value of a dollar?" As an adult, you must be financially responsible with money, the fruit of your labor. How is this done? You must create a workable, budgeted plan.

What is the spending plan for your monthly income? Create a budget to spend and save earnings. Take control!

Each employer compensates his or her employees according to the hours worked during a specific pay period. How often will you receive a paycheck? There are four basic pay schedules/pay dates. Direct deposit is when the

Figure 3-©Keith Bell/Shutterstock

companies deposit employees' paychecks into their bank accounts, credit union, or the financial institution of choice.

Possible paycheck payment schedules:

1. Weekly - Once a week, usually every Friday
2. Bi-Weekly- Every other Thursday or Friday (*Bonus* - In two months of the year, three paychecks are given. The yearly calendar determines when this occurs.)
3. Monthly – Once a month, usually the 1st or 30th of the month
4. Bi-Monthly- Twice a month, which is usually on the 1st and 15th or 15th and 30th of every month
5. Per Diem – Per day

Per Diem is a Latin term that means per day. Payment is given each day for time worked.

Bonus pay is additional money given to employees above their salary. One of the main reasons for a bonus is to say thank you, and other reasons include great job performance, sales commission, a contracted obligation, or the sharing in a company's great progress. Not all jobs give their employees bonuses, and the amount is not always the same each time. Do not rely on bonuses as part of your yearly salary. They are an extra financial gift, and they are not always given.

When a raise in salary comes about, save all or a portion of the additional funds, pay off debts, and splurge a little. Before your raise, hopefully, you were able to live off the previous salary, so save or invest the excess.

Tax Day

There are two experiences everyone is sure to have in life—death and taxes. April 15th is Tax Day in the United States. Federal, state, and city governments require each citizen to reconcile earned income during the previous year via filing tax forms. In the event of overpaid taxes, a refund is sent. If not enough taxes were paid, those monetary funds must be sent by midnight April 15th to the respective governmental agencies. (The April 15th due date is changed if not on a business day.)

Tax Preparation software assists in the process and will also give you an option to file taxes online. A professional tax preparer will also prepare your documents for a fee. In

MARLENE JENKINS COOPER

preparation for filing taxes, keep receipts for medical, charitable giving, employment and investment earnings, unemployment earnings, any income, and losses. These documents should be held for seven years before destroying them. Do not wait until the last minute to file your taxes. Late filings incur a financial penalty if money is owed.

Needs and Wants

What do you actually need to survive life each month, along with your added wants? At this point only, there are no wrong answers. Complete exercises 3A and 3B.

Money Tip

If your income is insufficient to pay monthly bills, find a better paying job, adjust your budget, and/or get an additional part-time job. Borrowing money to make up the deficiency is not an option.

Exercise #3A: List Your Top 10 Needs

1. _____

2. _____

3. _____

4. _____

5. _____

6. _____

7. _____

8. _____

9. _____

10. _____

Exercise #3B: List Your Top 10 Wants

1. _____

2. _____

3. _____

4. _____

5. _____

6. _____

7. _____

8. _____

9. _____

10. _____

Needs

There are four monthly basic necessities for survival. Firstly, a person should make these four basic needs a priority from their income. These basic needs are:

1.   Food
2.   Housing (rent/mortgage)
3.   Utilities
4.   Transportation
          (car or public transportation)

Money is necessary to provide for your needs. Needs are those things that you cannot live without. Your income should be able to cover all of your expenses. If not, adjust your budget and spending. Life's basic needs or essentials are food, shelter, and transportation. Food is needed for nourishment and survival. A place to call home is a major need. After the housing is acquired, specific utilities are needed to live adequately in the living space. Utilities include heat, water, gas, and electricity. These are basic needs, and everything else is a want. I did not forget clothes. You do not have to purchase new clothes every month in order to survive, although you may beg to differ. During the recent COVID-19 pandemic in early 2020, the government closed all non-essential businesses. All clothing stores were closed; clothes were not deemed essential. What happens to the rest of the money after all your needs are met?

Wants

Wants are those monthly items and experiences that we desire in our life that are not a part of the four basic needs. Wants include, but are not limited to cable television, cell phones, vacations, beauty/barber shop visits, gym memberships, clubs, podcasts, movies and streaming subscriptions, fraternity/sorority dues, entertainment, and other "stuff."

Revisit Exercises 3A and 3B with your newfound knowledge and re-evaluate your written responses to make the necessary changes.

Remember the four basic needs: housing, transportation, food, and utilities. Needs will most always remain the same, but needs may change and vary with life stages and lifestyles. It is wonderful to have a list of wants, but the wants must be affordable and fit into your budget. Random verbal statements from sale agents, cashiers, family, friends, and strangers, and even from yourself are, "You deserve it!" "You've earned it!" "Treat yourself!" "Retail therapy!" "You owe it to yourself," and "I want it now!" These statements may be true, but these statements can lead to deep financial trouble. Do these purchases fit into your budgetary plan? Many of my wants are purchased on Craigslist and eBay at an extreme price reduction. I have saved so much money buying new or gently used items from others.

Comparative shopping is a strategy to assist with purchasing an item or service for the lowest possible price. For example, the same product and same item number can have five or more different price points according to where the item is purchased. Use internet browsers and the plethora of apps on smartphones, iPad, tablets, and computers to assist with researching items when comparative shopping to find the lowest price. Unless saving money is not paramount in your mind, comparative shopping is a must!

Immediate or instant gratification can be costly and can lead you down a path of indebtedness. Wait! Delayed gratification does not mean denied forever. Resist impulse buying, and instead budget, plan, and save for your wants, which are not necessary for basic living.

Bills

A bill is a written financial statement for items and services used and/or purchased. When you make a purchase, your obligation is to pay it. Recurring bills usually come every month, and they include rent, gas, mortgage, utilities, and electricity. Some of these bills have fixed amounts every month and sometimes they vary. For example, your rent will remain the same until you get a rate increase. However, a heating bill is based on gas or electricity usage, and it is often lowered in the summer months. Other bills may come quarterly (every three months) or annually (once a year). There are many ways to pay a bill.

> 1. The old-fashioned way is to pay the bill by using a personal check or money order and placing it in the United States Postal Mail.
> 2. Pay in person with cash, personal check, credit card, or money order.
> 3. Pay the bill online via the company's website.4. Use your bill payment center at your bank or credit union using your bank account.
> 5. Send bill money by text via your cellphone.
> 6. Pay bills using phone or computer apps.

Money Tip
Pay bills before they are due! Do not wait!

Why should you pay bills? It is a moral and financial obligation to pay for purchases and/or services used. When a bill is sent, they give a specific date for payment, although the company may give a 15–28 day grace period. Some companies want their payment at a specific time of day on that date. For example, by 5:00 PM EST. Late payments usually incur late fees, so it is a good habit to pay bills before they are due.

Have a specific day(s) and time to pay bills each month. The worst-case scenario is to have enough money in the budget and bank account to pay the bills, but because of forgetfulness and lack of planning, the bills are paid late or not at all.

If offered, sign up for text or email due date reminders from bill companies. Use printed or online calendars to assist with noting reminders for all bill payments. Automated bill paying each month is another method to pay bills on time.

If the money is in the account to pay bills, there is no reason to wait until the bill's due date for payment. For some reason, some people have anxiety while paying bills. One of my students told the class that her mother curses every month while paying the household bills.

When there is a budgeted plan and spending is according to that plan, the plan should help alleviate some anxiety. Anxiety sometimes occurs when people do not have the funds to pay their bills and have no idea where the money will come from to pay the bills. Imagine when the bills arrive at your doorstep and you are unable to pay them. Or imagine the bills arriving at your doorstep and you pay them with the money allocated for them. Yes!!

Living paycheck to paycheck also creates anxiety. It's difficult to have calmness and stability if there are no usable funds left between paychecks. In the event of a lost job, an emergency fund will assist with expenses until the next job.

Reasons to Pay Bills on Time

1. Paying bills on time creates and sustains a good credit rating.
2. Bills paid late often incur a financial penalty. This penalty varies from company to company.
3 Late paid bills are often reported to the major credit bureaus: Experian, TransUnion, and Equifax.
4. Paying bills on time gives a creditworthy rating, except for those whose debt to credit ratio is high.

Credit Bureaus

Credit bureaus gather financial information about all of the monetary transactions by consumers. Each creditor reports the payment history of each consumer to one or more of the three major credit reporting agencies, Experian, TransUnion, and Equifax. These credit bureaus then create a credit report for everyone who has a credit history. Request a free credit report from the major credit bureaus to check your financial credit history and score. Notify the credit bureaus if any inaccuracies, fraudulent activity, or mistakes are listed in the report. To have a credit history, one must borrow and pay bills. Always maintain a good credit report. There is no law that you must borrow money!

The FICO Score

FICO is another company that determines a consumer's creditworthiness. FICO stands for Fair Isaac Corporation. A FICO score is a rating that calculates a consumer's debt, payment history, and debt to income ratio. This company determines a score based on payment history, the amount owed, length of credit history, new credit, and credit mix.[8] Usually, the higher the score, the lower the interest charged by banks, insurance companies, and loan corporations. A FICO score is used to determine insurance rates, interest rates for cars, houses, phones, and the renting of apartments. Unless a store or company does not report your financial paying habits, these habits and history cannot be hidden.

The FICO score can affect major purchases that need financing, like houses, boats, cars, apartment leases, and employment. Some employers run a background check of a potential employee's FICO scores and some insurance companies also check FICO scores before they insure an individual. Finally, many landlords check FICO scores before leasing apartments. Low scores equal high risk, and high scores equal low risk. Four types of credit ratings include poor, fair, good, and excellent. Most lenders want people who pay their bills on time and who are creditworthy!

---

[8] "How Are FICO Scores Calculated? | MyFICO | MyFICO", n.d., Accessed September 7, 2020. https://www.myfico.com/credit-education/whats-in-your-credit-score.

What's Your Score?

Congratulations!! You've found the car of your dreams! The car purchase price is $30,000.00, with a down payment of $2,000.00, and the balance of $28,000 must be financed. Who will finance the loan? Will the credit union, bank, other financial institution, or your loving parents finance the loan? What would happen to our economy if everyone paid his or her car in full with cash when purchasing a car? The lending agencies would not make any money.

No law states that you must purchase a brand-new car. As soon as a new car is driven off the car lot, the car depreciates by 10 percent. Certified used cars or purchasing an excellent used car from a private person can be great options.

Personal financed car payments are based on your FICO score or the credit report from one of the three major credit bureaus. Each company uses their scoring criteria.

For example, the FICO scores below determine the financed interest rates on a car payment monthly cost:

800+	Excellent
740- 799	Good
580- 669	Fair score
579 and lower	Poor score

Usually, interest rates for purchases are based on FICO scores, and the higher the FICO score, the lower the monthly costs. Knowing the above information before making large purchases will assist with the buying process. Payments and interest rates are based on personal credit scores. A free credit report is due to every person each person. Check for scores, fraudulent activity, and any mistakes listed on the report.

Debt

What is debt? Debt is borrowing money from anyone to pay for anything! The unspoken mantra for those who borrow is "I want it now, and I will pay for it later." Debt is spending other people's money because usually the cash is not available or you are making a choice to not use personal funds. Having a credit card from any company that is not paid off each month in full is carrying debt! Buying a phone on installments is buying with debt. Do not create debt! Live within your means and live on a budget. Do not spend more money than you make each month.

Co-signing helps someone else get a loan that is not creditworthy. As a co-signer, the signature on the legal document states that the co-signer will finish paying the loan if the first signer defaults, stops paying the loan, or dies. Once the document is signed, the co-signer is forever financially responsible until the loan is paid off.

Money Tip
Never co-sign for anyone to get a loan!

Life Lesson
Pay your bills on time.

Credit Cards & Student Loans

Why are we talking about debt? According to Northwestern Mutual's 2020 Planning and Progress Study, the average American has $26,621 in debt, which does not include a mortgage.[9] I hope at this point in your life, you are not starting your adult life with debt. However, many young adults start adulthood with large amounts of student loan debt and/or credit card debt. This may not be your story, but there needs to be a discussion about debt.

According to Matt Frankel and Kamran Rosen, authors of the article "Credit Card Debt Statistics for 2020," at the beginning of 2020, Americans had an average of 4 credit cards each with an average total balance of 6,194.00.[10]

Debt is spending other people's money because usually the cash at the time of purchase or service is not in your bank account. Therefore, many companies and banks will lend the borrower their money and charge a fee for doing so. One terrible way to borrow money is purchasing items and/or services via a credit card. If you financially qualify and a company deems you responsible to pay the money back, a company will allow you to make purchases under its name and/or advance money for a

---

[9] Newsroom | Northwestern Mutual – Planning and Progress Study 2019", n.d., Accessed September 7, 2020. https://news.northwesternmutual.com/planning-and-progress-2019.

[10] "Credit Card Debt Statistics for 2020 | The Ascent", n.d., Accessed January 15, 2020. https://www.fool.com/the-ascent/research/credit-card-debt-statistics/.

price with fees. This should not be the preferred way to acquire money that you have not earned! Earn the money first, unless you can pay off the balance before it is due. Never let a credit card balance roll over to the next month's bill. Pay off the credit card bill in full every month.

Getting out of debt should be the number one priority, and planning for retirement should be priority number two. If in financial trouble, plan to get rid of the debt as soon as possible. Be wary of companies that give interest-free loans for any amount of years, or companies that promise you a product can be yours for just four easy payments. Missed or late payments increase the interest rate to astronomical high-interest rates. For example, I purchased a dryer from a major department store with an interest-free loan for three months. For my last payment, I waited for the due date and wanted to pay online. However, some companies do not immediately post online payments. When I called the customer service department, the clerk could not confirm that I would be credited for my payment on that given day. Since I knew the high penalty for late payment, I went to the mall and made the payment in person. If the payment was posted a day later, I would have been charged the converted high interest rate for the entire three months. If only I paid the bill days earlier, this situation would not have been a problem. I flirted with financial danger. Read the fine print on the agreement, especially about the time period in which you receive 0% interest. Buy what is affordable with cash!

For those with student loan debt, the debt must be paid! "Out of sight, out of mind" cannot be applied to student loans. Bankruptcy via Chapter 7, Chapter 11, or Chapter 13 will not dismiss student loan debt. The repayment of student loans will never go away unless one becomes fully disabled or die; otherwise, the debt must be paid.

If in debt, plan to get out now! If possible, pay more than the minimum amount on the billing statement every month. There are websites, debt payoff apps, and debt online calculators to assist with a plan for getting out of debt. The burden of debt is a heavy load. Lift the burden and live debt-free!

The Credit Card

In 2019, the estimated average amount of credit card debt for Americans is $6,849.[11] Listed below are six major credit card issuers that are widely used for purchases at most businesses.

---

[11] "American Household Credit Card Debt Statistics: 2019 – NerdWallet", n.d., Accessed September 8, 2020. https://www.nerdwallet.com/blog/average-credit-card-debt-household/.

They are:

1. MasterCard
2. Visa
3. American Express
4. Chase
5. Citibank
6. Discover Card

Having an owed balance from any company that is not paid off each month in full is called debt! Do not use credit cards unless you can pay the total monthly balance off each month! This takes discipline and planning. Some people have more than one credit card, others have ten or more, and some have none. The alternative to using a credit card is using a debit card. A debit card uses cash that is in your bank account. A credit card is borrowed money and a debit card uses cash linked to a personal bank account.

Use your hard-earned money and no one else's to pay for expenses. Have power over your money and spend it wisely! Live within your means. In fact, try to live below your means. Do not use other people's money to live the life you want to live. Live on less than you earn. Save for those special items and experiences you want. Pay credit cards by the due date. Failure to pay credit cards on time will result in huge penalties, fees, and potential bad credit ratings.

Debt offers upon debt offers for borrowing money show up in the United States postal mail, emails, phone calls, in-store promotions, texts, and anywhere possible. Companies want people to believe money is easily accessible. They say, "I can help fulfill all your desires, now." Whatever happened to restraint? Whatever happened to saving for wanted items? Many say, "No, I want it now!" The I-want-it-now philosophy, or instant gratification, has put millions and millions of people in debt. Some people who have $20,000 in credit card debt and do not even have a clue what they owe. Why do people in debt take their friends out to dinner and incur additional debt by placing the dinner tab on their credit card with high interest rates? No judgment, but does that make sense?

Companies want consumers to spend their hard-earned money. There are analytics on buyers' spending habits. Flash sales on Instagram, flash sales via text messages, television ads, and Facebook ads keep the pressure to spend high. Buy what is affordable in your budget. Once again! Do not create debt! Live within your means! Live on a budget and spend less than you make each month. Consumers will be tempted by many credit card companies, banks, insurance companies, department stores, and the like with offers to open and apply for credit card and store accounts. Some credit card companies offer zero interest rates for a year or more. I recently received one in the mail, and I began to think of what I could purchase with the interest-free money. Be careful! Reject those thoughts and letters! Destroy, delete, or shred the invitation to debt letters in the United States postal mail or email.

Never pay the minimum payments on credit cards. It will take a lifetime to pay off the debt. If you can, add extra money to your monthly minimum payments. According to the Federal Reserve, only 45% of US cardholders pay their credit card balances in full monthly.[12] Do not ignore your debt by not paying the monthly payments or not opening the mail. The bill will not disappear. Years ago, while married, I figured if I did not open the credit card bills, they would go away. Of course, they did not go away, but instead the account racked up additional fees and costs. I finally opened the letters after some time and started paying them with the added penalties and fees. Pay your bill; I sadly did not. I finally paid the credit card balance. Do not ignore your financial obligations. Lesson learned.

After college, many are bogged down with student loan debt. If this is the case, do not create any more debt. Governmental backed student loans (Sallie Mae) and some private educational loans will become due shortly after you graduate. Whether you

---

[12] "American Household Credit Card Debt Statistics: 2019 – NerdWallet", n.d., Accessed September 8, 2020. https://www.nerdwallet.com/blog/average-credit-card-debt-household/.

have graduated or not, be ready to pay the loans monthly until they are paid off. Graduate from school!

There are two types of debt, secured and unsecured. Secured debt is debt that is attached to collateral. For example, a house or car is collateral. If you default on your loan or do not pay the monthly bill, the company will foreclose on your house or repossess your car. Unsecured debt is a loan without collateral attached to it.

Do not let debt ruin your credit. Pay your bills and do not borrow money. Good debt and bad debt were terms used by many. In years past, good debt included educational and vocational costs and a home mortgage. However, in the 21st Century, student debt has financially crippled many people because of the costs of attending college. Therefore, student loans are no longer known as good debt. To manage student loan debt, contact your loan officer, university financial aid department, and/or the bank. Bad debt is having credit card balances, personal loans, purchasing consumable items and things that depreciate without using funds. If finances trouble your life, get a plan to get out of debt.

The Car

For some people, owning an automobile is a necessity. For others who live in a municipality like New York City, Philadelphia, Washington, or Baltimore, where public transportation is available and adequate, a car is not a necessity.

If you need a car in your twenties and cannot afford a new car, an older used car will do. My community calls those types of cars "Hoopties." A brand-new Mercedes and a 2015 Honda CR-V will both take you to work! Do not get into extreme car debt over a late model car payment. It is a wonderful feeling not to have to pay a car note each month. Some people save and pay for a car with cash; this is the best financial option.

If you must finance a car, here are some tips on buying a new car or a certified used car.

Car Buying Tips

When car shopping, research, research, and do additional research on the makes and models of the potential new or used car. Know the process of what to do and not to do when purchasing a car from car dealers. Never pay the sticker price that is on the car window. Know your credit score and credit rating before shopping for a car.

Negotiate! Negotiate and negotiate some more to acquire the desired car at the desired price. If the negotiated price is not satisfactory, walk away from the negotiations, go home, and maybe come back the next day to negotiate some more. This may or may not work in your favor, but it is a negotiating tactic. If additional research is needed while at the negotiating table, use a smartphone or iPad to gather research. Lots of numbers and information will be given, so be prepared. Each car salesperson is trained and skilled in the art of selling and negotiating to benefit him/her and the car dealership. Another method of purchasing a car is via the internet via car dealerships' websites in your area. Request an internet price for the specific car you want.

While negotiating, if a pre-approved car loan letter or the check from the bank or credit union is in your pocket, keep that information from the salesperson. Why? Also, if your present car is dying and is near death's door, keep that information to yourself. Keep your final best price to yourself, but know what that price is. Why? The salesperson has additional sales tactics for each of those scenarios with that information. Giving away pertinent information sometimes gives the salesperson leverage in making the sale.

If at all possible, women should take a man knowledgeable in buying cars with them to the dealership and negotiating table. I agree that some women can out-negotiate men, but we live in a male-dominated world. When the negotiated price has been agreed upon, carefully review the final car transaction paperwork multiple times before signing on the dotted line.

If financing a car, the loan should be for no more than three years. The monthly car note payments, including car insurance and maintenance costs, should be no more than 10-15 percent of your take-home pay. An informed, knowledgeable buyer can save a great deal on his or her purchase.

As soon as you leave the car lot with your brand-new car, the car depreciates from 7- 11 percent and maybe more. Consider purchasing gap insurance if financing a car. Gap insurance protects you in case of a total loss if there is a car accident. Based on your down payment, your car loan may be more than the car's worth at the time of the accident. It is still your responsibility to pay the car off in case of a total loss. Gap insurance will fill in the gap between what you owe and what the car's worth at the time of the accident.

At 30 years old, my two-income family purchased a wonderful, brand-new 1987 Volvo sedan. The monthly car note, maintenance, and car insurance were extremely high, but I loved that car. Those costs ate up my family's budget each month. Big mistake! And where is the car now? Never again!

Follow the tips below for great car care.

Basic Car Maintenance Tips

1. Get oil and filter changes according to the manufacturer's recommendations or every 3000-5000 miles for older cars.
2. Always keep at least a quarter tank of gas in your car.
3. Keep tires inflated to the manufacturer's recommended tire pressure. Rotate and balance tires every 3000 – 5000 miles.
4. Check transmission fluid, antifreeze, and engine oil levels. Learn how to do this.
5. Use a reputable car mechanic for repairs.
Check your car manual for specific instructions on the above tips.

In case your car malfunctions, subscribe to a 24-hour emergency roadside service like American Automobile Association (AAA) or a car dealer's emergency roadside service. Always keep an emergency car kit in the car, which includes a blanket, bottled water, ice scraper and snow brush, nuts (unless allergic), flashlight and batteries, phone charger, phone battery that's fully charged, flares, and first aid kit. Add additional items according to your needs. Old magazines are in my emergency car kit because I do not like to be bored when waiting for emergency roadside service. Winter items can be removed from the car during the spring, summer, and fall months. Put those items back during the fall, according to the severity of your winter months.

Vacations/Travel

Are vacations affordable? Yes, but vacations must be planned, budgeted, and saved for in advance. Why wait until retirement to travel?

A vacation can be one or more of the following:

1. A new adventure at a new destination
2. Another place to relax
3. An educational experience at a conference, workshop, or convention
4. A family time experience away from home
5. Respite from the everyday routine

Lengths of vacations:

1. An overnight stay
2. A weekend getaway
3. A week
4. Two weeks
5. A month or more
6. Thirty days
7. The entire summer

The Price of a Vacation

Many senior citizens state that they want to travel when they retire. Why wait? Travel now! Save, budget for travel, read, research, get reviews, and read some more on possible travel destinations, go where you can afford to go, and pay for the vacation before leaving on it. There are travel groups, friends who like to travel, family trips, and solo trips. Have a valid passport!

Mark A. Cooper II, in his book, *The Power of the Passport,* states, "It's great to see landmarks and works of art that you envisioned when you were younger, but for me, the true bonus is in getting to meet the people of the country and embracing their culture."[13]

The Cost of Vacations

1. Inexpensive/ No Frills
2. Budget Friendly
3. Average
4. Expensive/Luxury
5. Last-minute bookings
6. Free

Types of Vacations

1. A La Carte - pay for each experience yourself, i.e., food, sports activities, tours, drinks.
2. All Inclusive - everything is paid for, including, lodging, food, excursions, entertainment, and drinks. Sometimes alcoholic drinks are not included.
3. All-inclusive except for excursions, tours, and alcoholic and soft drinks.
4. All-Inclusive Packages - everything is included, even the airfare.
5. Staycation - staying in your home city or town but going to a hotel or bed and breakfast.
6. Spending time with family who live away from your hometown or state.
7. A conference combined with a vacation.

---

[13] Cooper, Mark A, *The Power of the Passport* (Philadelphia: Songs of Judah Publishing, 2019) 5.

Tipping

When planning a trip, you must never forget to tip the people that give you personal service during your vacation. Tipping occurs after the service is satisfactorily completed. The rule of thumb for luggage is $2.00 per bag. Tipping is personal, but there are standard rates. Fifteen to twenty percent is the standard tipping rule for most services. At all costs, try to rectify any problems with service before tipping a lower amount.

Let's experience the tipping path for traveling on vacation only.

And the Tip Goes To...

Scenario 1

This vacation is for two persons traveling by airplane to Bermuda. Each person has one suitcase and a carry-on. (Prices may vary per location.)

A. Leaving the house for the airport

1. Rideshare/Taxi/Shuttle Van driver	$8.00
2. Airport baggage handler to shuttle/taxi-van to hotel	$8.00
3. Rideshare/Taxi/Shuttle Van driver	$8.00
4. Bell Hop to your hotel room or villa	$8.00
Total	$32.00

B. Return to home

1. Bell Hop to from hotel room or villa to shuttle van	$8.00
2. Shuttle Van driver to the airport	$8.00
3. Airport baggage handler to Uber driver/airport shuttle van	$8.00
4. Uber driver/airport shuttle van to home	$8.00

Total	$32.00

Grand Total Travel Tips $64.00

Is there another way to do the above? Yes, there is.

Scenario 2
Two persons going to Bermuda by airplane with one suitcase each and a carry-on each.

A. Leaving the house for the airport-

1. Uncle Joey drives you to the airport	$0.00
2. Take the luggage into the airport yourself	$0.00
3. Airport shuttle van/taxi driver to hotel	$8.00
4. Take your luggage to the hotel room	$0.00

Total	$8.00

B. Return to home

1. Bring your own luggage to hotel lobby	$0.00
2. Shuttle Van/taxi driver to airport	$8.00
3. Take the luggage into the airport yourself	$0.00
4. Take the luggage from baggage claim to the car	$0.00
5. Uncle Joey drives you home	$0.00

Total	$8.00

Grand Total Travel Tips $16.00

Life's Unexpected Problems

Unexpected, unforeseen, and unplanned expenses sometimes occur when least expected. Emergencies come when we least expect it. Money is usually needed to meet an emergency. You might think that if money is not available, borrowing is a quick fix. No, no, no! Have a backup plan for the unexpected. An emergency fund should have 3-6 months of expenses saved in case of emergencies. Another name for an emergency fund is "A Rainy Day Fund."

In Henry Wadsworth Longfellow's poem "Rainy Days," the famous 19th century poet said, "Into each life some rain must fall." The problem is, we do not know when. Troubles do happen. There are often hints, warnings, and indicators that something may break or malfunction, but no one knows the exact time. Also, there are times when there are no warnings, and an item just breaks or a sickness occurs. Plan in advance for such emergencies. An emergency fund for life's unexpected problems will be a safety net. When Rainy Day Emergency Funds are used, as soon as possible, replace the money for other future emergencies.

Financial hardships may arise. Losing a job, having a medical emergency, furloughed, pandemic, and/or a major malfunction in the home or car can create a major financial hardship, but having an adequate emergency fund will help alleviate some of the burdens and sustain you until the emergency ends.

Plan for Possible Future Emergencies!

Sample of Unexpected / Unplanned Events

(The following list is not conclusive.)

Job loss / layoff	Car accident
Debilitating sickness	House fire
Spouse leaves for the military	Inflation
Gas prices rise	Rising heating cost
Expensive medication	Broken washing machine
Refrigerator stops working	Faulty car transmission
Laid off from job	Governmental shutdown
Union strike on job	Water heater breaks
Separation or divorce	Tutoring costs for children
Furloughed	Pandemic

Life's Unexpected Problems

Exercise #4: The Emergency

Choose one of the above problems and write how you will handle it. What are your options? You may ask others for help, but hopefully not for a loan or gift. No credit card use!

_____

_____

_____

Insurance

In the sample personal budget below, insurance is listed as a line item. Insurance is monetary help/aid for the "just in case" of an accident, breakage, or a malfunction of an item. Insurance is available for humans and animals for wellness and health problems. However, a monetary premium or a cost must be paid before the unfortunate happens to be insured. Although the unfortunate may never happen, the assurance of having insurance is financial security for the "just-in-case."

Insurance premiums are paid yearly, monthly, or quarterly. Premiums can be costly, but the premiums are part of the process. Allow room for premiums in your monthly budget. Be intentional on adequately insuring each item for replacement costs or the cost to fix the item.

There are many types of insurance, and they are as follows:

1. Health insurance
2. Car insurance
3. House/Renters insurance
4. Pet insurance
5. Flood insurance
6. Life insurance
7. Dental insurance
8. Prescription insurance
9. Vision (eye) insurance
10. Appliance/furniture insurance
11. Gap insurance
12. Long-term care

Each type of insurance has a written policy agreement that will state what is covered in the agreement. When using insurance, remember that most insurance has a deductible or co-payment (co-pay) in order to use the coverage of the insurance. A deductible or co-pay is money that will come out of the insured's pocket. These costs can vary according to the policy.

Carefully read the policy before signing and purchasing the insurance. Also read the fine print. Know and understand what is and is not covered in the policies. For example, you can have house insurance, but the policy may not cover flooding. Additional separate insurance called flood insurance may be needed when living in a flood zone. Speak to an insurance agent and be clear what is covered before purchasing the insurance. Ask parents, family, and friends who are knowledgeable for assistance in this area.

Some employers and companies pay their employees' health, dental, vision, and life insurance premiums or a portion of it, and the employee pays the other portion. Often, the insured (that's you) is required to co-pay every time the insurance is used. Not all health care benefits are covered. Check your health coverage documents.

Do I need health insurance? When a sickness arises, are the out-of-pocket payments affordable to pay the doctor and/or hospital fees? Are wellness visits and annual checkups affordable? Can my budget pay health insurance each month, quarterly, or yearly? I believe health insurance is necessary if you can afford the premiums. Many Americans cannot afford to pay monthly health insurance premiums or co-pays because health insurance can be very expensive. Hospital costs, doctor fees, and costs related to hospital services have landed many people in debt because of their inability to pay the bill for their hospital stay, operation, and related costs.

Do I need to purchase all of the above types of insurance? No! However, if you have a fire in your home, can you afford to replace the structure and the contents of the house without help from an insurance policy? If someone robs your apartment, can you replace the contents of the apartment that were stolen? If you hit another car or someone hits your car that does not have insurance, can you fix or replace your car with your savings or emergency fund? Purchase and choose the insurances that are necessary to meet your lifestyle. Please note: Keep your insurance policies paid and up to date. If premiums are not paid within the grace period, the insurance policy will lapse; in other words, canceled. Life insurance obtained via your job is sometimes canceled when you leave their employment.

Quarterly Bills

For quarterly bills, save money in advance for those bills that are not monthly. I save for my quarterly bills in specific accounts at my credit union, i.e. taxes, seasonal bills, bi-yearly life insurances. These quarterly bills can be a budget line item or budget for them in the miscellaneous category.

Clothing

In the biblical days of Adam and Eve, clothes were not needed. In the 21st century in America, however, everyone needs clothes to cover their body parts. That being said, purchasing new clothes every month is not a necessity. If I were to look into your closet right now, what would I find? Are there clothes in three different sizes in the closet? For ladies, do you have 5 or more skirts of the same color or texture? How many black skirts or dresses does a lady need? For men and women, how many pairs of blue denim jeans, pairs of shoes, and sneakers are in your closet?

Take inventory of all the clothes and shoes in your house. Ask the question, "Is each item needed?" Get rid of those clothes that are damaged and do not fit properly, and donate unwanted clothes to charitable organizations that sell them in thrift shops or have giveaways. Another alternative is to sell unneeded clothes on eBay, Craigslist, and at garage sales.

Clothing Tip

Every time a clothing item and/or a pair of shoes is purchased, take another item from the closet and give it away. Rid yourself of an older clothing item.

71

Children constantly grow, and they will outgrow their clothes on a consistent basis, and these clothes will need to be replaced. Budget for children's clothing in your monetary plan.

For adult clothing, use your budget plan to purchase new clothes. No law states that new clothes must be purchased each month. If there is not a reason to purchase clothes in a particular month, save the budgeted clothing allowance and add it to next month's budget.

Identity Theft

Protect yourself from thieves who try to steal your personal information for their personal financial gain, which can be obtained through you, the internet, and print documents. Keep your passwords, Social Security number, bank information, and birthdate private. When finished with personal documents and bank information, please do not throw them in the trash; shred them! Be suspicious of people who call on the phone and pretend to be from a reputable company. Do not give out your highly sensitive personal information on the phone. If someone steals your personal information, notify the police, your credit card companies, credit bureaus, and check all financial accounts. Check your credit report to see if unauthorized accounts have been opened. Beware and be careful!

CHAPTER 4

Breaking Down the Budget Line Item by Line Item

I can do this! I can win with money. Now that a steady full-time job has been acquired with a hopefully adequate income, how will you manage the money from your paycheck? A key element in financial management is a personal budget. Financial wellness is always our goal.

Who does the money belong to? The money belongs to you, and it is your job to properly manage it. Your name is on the paycheck. I have already told you to imagine your employer putting your parent's name(s) on your paycheck. This would upset you. Your paycheck is the result of your hard-earned work. Use a budget plan to help with great money management skills.

What is the budget? A personal budget is a written financial plan that sets and tracks your income and expenses for a time period, usually yearly, and then is broken down monthly. A personal budget is a window into a person's finances, documenting where the money is going, has gone, or will go. With wise planning, place the money in the budget where you want it to go with a purpose.

Another term for a budget is a money management plan. With your lifestyle in mind, personally design your money management plan. There are some boundaries one should have when setting up a money management plan or budget. For example, one should not spend more than twenty-five percent of their monthly take-home income on an apartment or a leased house. Spend as little as you can on your monthly car expenses. For many, a car is necessary, but make sure to drive one that is affordable. Renting or purchasing items that are unaffordable, such as luxury apartments, cars, or houses is a terrible mistake.

Will there be any money left at the end of the month from your paycheck? Is it possible to run out of money before the end of the month? Can I save some money from each paycheck? Is my spending out of control? How do I handle a lack of funds at the end of the month? What are your answers to these questions?

Some old folks state, "There is sometimes more month than money." Others say, "I'm living month to month." Others say, "I'm living paycheck to paycheck." In a 2019 survey completed by The First Bank of Omaha, their findings stated that forty-nine percent of Americans say that they are living paycheck to paycheck and only fifty-three percent have an emergency fund.[14] These numbers are disheartening, but with careful budget planning, it is possible to make it to the end of the month with your income. These numbers do not give us permission to be in the above group. With careful planning, you can make it to the end of the month with your strategic budget plan. Sometimes a new part-time job or cutting down some expenses might be necessary.

Many people are struggling month to month to make ends meet. Some of this struggle is due to having an insufficient or inadequate income, and others who might normally have a sufficient income do not wisely spend it. First, have a monthly budget plan. Second, do not spend more money than your paycheck brings in. Use coupons, cut back on spending, get a part-time job, further your education level, and/or find a better paying job. There are options!

The percentages stated below on spending are flexible within reason. However, the percentage limits are stated, but feel free to lower the percentages. Housing percentages should be no more than 25% of the take-home pay (post taxes). Any housing percentage over the 25% amount is unaffordable. If

---

[14] "Nearly Half of Americans Live Paycheck to Paycheck: Bank Survey", n.d., Accessed February 20, 2020. https://www.washingtonexaminer.com/news/nearly-half-americans-live-paycheck-to-paycheck-bank-survey.

transportation expenses, including gas, car payment, and maintenance are above 20%, the car is not affordable.

Imagine this! If a person spends 25% on housing and 25% for transportation, the budget is only left with an additional 50 percent for other expenses. Can this be done? The budget percentages must add up to one hundred percent. Do the math, and good luck.

Budget Percentages

Housing	20-25%
Health Insurance	10-25%
Food	10-15%
Transportation	10-15%
Utilities	5-10%
Savings	10-15%
Entertainment	5-10%
Clothes	5-7%
Spending Money	5-10%
Miscellaneous	5-10%
Charitable Giving	10%

Therefore, one's budget cannot be fully based on the higher end of all of the above personal budget percentages. However, the lower end of all of the above percentages is 95%, so there is an additional 5% to go higher on a category. If the above percentage amounts are more than 100 percent, carefully decide what you need to lower. For instance, maybe the vacation cruise to Australia will not be taken this year. Instead, a weekend trip to a nearby resort will be the yearly vacation. The consequences of not using a budgetary plan could be devastating to your financial health. There are many types of budget plans, but I subscribe to the above one.

Often, people who do not use a budget ask this old age question: "Where did all the money go?" Another well-known expression is, "Money burns a hole in your pocket." This can happen if you do not have a plan for the income you earn. These people cannot save or keep the money. A personal budget maps out a detailed statement on where your money will go each month.

.

Money Tips
Live on less than you earn.
Live within your means.
Live and spend on purpose.

However, budgets may and will have to be modified based on circumstances, good, bad, and unforeseen. For example, high temperatures will raise your electric bill when using air conditioners or central air conditioning at full operating speed.

Or very low temperatures will raise the gas/electric heating bill. Daycare, summer camp, and/or overnight camp tuition must be added to your family budget for June, July, and August. However, save for this the entire year.

A zero balanced budget must reflect the destination of every dollar of the income. A zero balanced budget means that the budget is at zero at the end of the month with each dollar going where it was told to go. A balanced budget is a budget where the expenses and income are not greater than or less than each other. If the budget is in the negative, more money was spent than earned and the budget is unbalanced. This is called, "Being in the red!" Where did my money go? "Being in the black" means that there has been no overspending of income funds, all the bills have been paid, and the money is not in the negative. Basically, this means that you know where the money went, there was no overspending, and that there is money left from the monthly budget.

While teaching the lesson on balancing a budget to my students, a highly frustrated young lady could not balance her budget no matter how she tried to fix it. She sat there frustrated and ready to cry. I let her sit there and figure it out. She had to make some difficult decisions and she did. A taste of reality goes a long way.

If there is not a spot in the budget plan for your money to go, the money will walk away to unnamed places with your permission. A budget plan needs to be in place to assist with spending income.

Unfortunate things can happen to your monthly budget. For example, some line items such as gas and electric costs change each month due to usage. If the weather has been uncharacteristically cold for several weeks and the heater has been pumping heat non-stop, heating costs for that month will increase. For that month, the regular heating bill may go from $150.00 to $250.00. How do you handle this? Borrowing from your parents or family is not an option. You are independent.

There are several options:

1. Lower the thermostat a few degrees and wear a sweater. (Be careful! Do not lower the thermostat too many degrees because the pipes may freeze.)

2. Use other discretionary money from the budget (clothing allowance, allowance money, or entertainment money). Take from "Peter to pay Paul." I will explain this more later.

3. Use $100.00 from the Emergency Fund.

Budgets will change based on your marital status, children, and/or additional dependents. A dependent is anyone who depends on someone else for their financial and living existence. Dependents can/could include your spouse, children, aged parents, or other family members.

The Budget

There are two major parts of a budget, income, and expenditures. The income is the monetary funds that come into your household each month. This can include any funds from first or second jobs, child support, revenue from stocks and bonds, and alimony. These funds come in every month. Expenditures or expenses are the funds that leave the budget each month. These expenditures include anything paid from the paycheck. The list is exhausting!

A budget can be created on paper, in a spreadsheet or a template, or in budget software or apps. Choose one or more above that suits you. A personal budget is personal to you. Therefore, if you use a template or budget software, you will have to modify the budget to meet your needs.

A spreadsheet is a computer program that allows you to calculate mathematical formulas based on imputed numerical data. The formulas complete the math computations. Just add the numbers and data.

Budget spreadsheets can be created and designed in Microsoft Excel, Open Office, or Google Sheets, and there are many free templates that come with these programs. Also, use the free or paid online budget spreadsheets that can be personalized. There are a plethora of basic sample budgets and budget templates online with a spreadsheet built into the

program. For example, consider mint.com and
everydaydollar.com.

Budgeting takes great discipline. Denying yourself things
not in the budget can be difficult. Save for wants. Impulse
buying and immediate gratification can often destroy a budget
plan, as well as creating debt. With that in mind, let's begin the
planning of the budget.

To have a budget, you must have an income—money
coming in! In the first section of your budget is income, and you
should list all streams of income. The next section is the
expenditures. List all your expenses. This section should be
divided into a needs and wants section.

The last item on the budget should be what money should be
left at the end of the budget. The number should compute to zero
(o). Why? After you subtract the expenditures from the income,
the remainder should be zero. Each dollar of the paycheck
should be assigned a spot in the personal budget. If not, the
money will go anywhere it chooses and you might never know
where. Money slips through your fingers without a destination.

A personal budget will assist with controlling spending. A
budget is not foolproof. Variables can attack a budget.
Temperatures can drop, you might have to take sick leave, or
there could be unexpected costs, price increases, and other
variables. Buying a new pocketbook that is not in the budget or
a new video game is not an acceptable variable. Control

yourself! Customize the personal budget below to meet your
needs.

Sample Generic Budget

Month -	Estimated	Actual
Income (Net)		
Primary Job		
Part-time Job		
Interest/Investments		
Total Income		
Expenditures—Needs		
Savings/ Emergency Fund		
Retirement Savings		
Tithe/ Charity		
Food		
Groceries		
Take Out - Restaurants		
Housing		
Rent/Mortgage		
HOA		
Rental-House Insurance		
Utilities		
Water		
Gas/Heat		
Electricity		
Transportation		
Car Note/Public/ Ride Share		
Gasoline		
Car Maintenance		
Car Insurance		
Childcare/Education		
Health Insurance		
Other-		

Month -	Estimated	Actual
Other-		
Total Needs Expenditures		
Expenditures—Wants		
Clothes		
Dental Insurance		
Life Insurance		
Cell Phone		
Cable TV		
Internet—Wi-Fi		
Student Loans		
Personal Care/Toiletries		
Credit Card #1		
Yearly Gift Giving		
December Holiday/Christmas Gifts		
Pet Care		
Gym Membership		
Hairdresser/Barber		
Vacation		
Allowance		
Subscriptions/Streaming		
Entertainment		
Miscellaneous		
Other		
Total Want Expenditures		
Total Needs & Wants Expenditures		
Total Money Left		

Other Types of Budgets

The budget has been established, but how will the money be handled? The envelope system and the money jar system are two systems that help with the budget process. In the envelope cash-only system, money from the paycheck is placed in specific envelopes. The envelopes include expenses, which will include rent, utilities, food, miscellaneous, savings, car, and allowance envelops.

In the money jar system, money from the paycheck is placed in regular glass jars for specific purposes. The author of *Secrets of the Millionaire Mind*, T. Harv Eker, has created a sophisticated JARS money management system that is based on the money jar system. His system places money in 6 jars—necessities, long term, education, play, financial, and giving. Both the envelope and the jar systems work for many people; others modify the process. Others find both systems difficult to operate. Find a system that works for you.

Savings

Just because an income comes into your life each month does not mean that the money has to leave your hands, wallet, pocket, or bank account every time you get paid. Spend less than you earn. Remember, it is not how much you earned, but how much you save. It is possible to earn a six-figure salary and be broke! How? By spending more than you earned!

Save at least 10-15% from monthly earnings. Gross or net you ask? This is your choice. Remember, the more you save, the more money you will have in your savings account. If ten percent is a stretch at this time, choose a lower percentage until it becomes achievable, but save! Have savings automatically deposited from the paycheck into your bank.

Why save? Many people do not believe in saving. "Live for today," they say, but that does not leave much money left to save. Did they never hear the saying, "Save for a rainy day?" Saving takes discipline. Here are five reasons why you should save:

Five Reasons Why You Should Save

1. Save for emergencies. We cannot predict the future. Only God knows the future. Murphy's Law states "Anything that can go wrong will go wrong." Save for unforeseen events.
2. Save for retirement. Our retirement money will multiply and gain interest in mutual funds, annuities, and retirement accounts for retired living later in life. (Remember, there are risks involved in any investment.)
3. Savings provide security, a cushion that puts our mind at ease in case of an unexpected financial event.
4. Save for items you would like to purchase in the future, i.e., car, house, or vacations.

5. Save for life events, i.e., weddings, anniversary parties, birth, and the raising of children.

Ways to Save

1. The easiest way to save is to have ten percent or more automatically deducted from your paycheck and placed in a savings account.
2. Save the change from your pockets and/or pocketbook and put it in a bottle, can, or container. Do not touch it.
3. Budget for your savings!
4. Use your nice, big, round piggy bank.

Although I have used each of the above methods of saving, the automatic saving withdrawal principal works best. However, leave the money in the savings account and do not touch it. Unfortunately, it is very easy to take from your savings and use it for other uses. Discipline is key! Do not touch the money.

Investments

Investing in mutual funds is a great way to grow earned income. A mutual fund is a group of diverse stocks in one portfolio managed by an investment company. Speak to a financial professional on how and where to invest money. Compound interest is an excellent way to grow money. From past performance, mutual fund investments usually double every twelve years. Leave the money alone in the account and do not touch it until the age 65 or needed for retirement. The stock market will go up and down, but if the money is left alone, it should double every twelve years. Just imagine doing this at twenty years old. Guess how much money is in the account at 65 years of age? Do the math!! Yes, compound interest is wonderful. I am very sorrowful that I did not do this in my twenties. Save early in life.

Allowance

Working, saving, and paying bills cannot be totally fun without having money in the budget to splurge. Budget and give yourself an allowance. Allowance is a matter of preference, but many want to have some fun with some of the earned income.

Banking

Where will the monetary funds be kept? Great grandmother may have kept her money under the mattress, but these days it is necessary to have a bank or credit union to deposit and withdraw monetary funds. Many employers electronically direct deposit employee paychecks into their bank accounts every pay period.

Many young adults do not have a checking account or even know how to write a check. Millennials often pay bills via their phones' apps, online, or in cash. For all practical purposes, information on writing a check is below. When writing a check, a check must be dated and signed by the issuer in cursive writing in a black or blue pen. The amount of the check has to be written and in numerical form.

Sample Personal Check

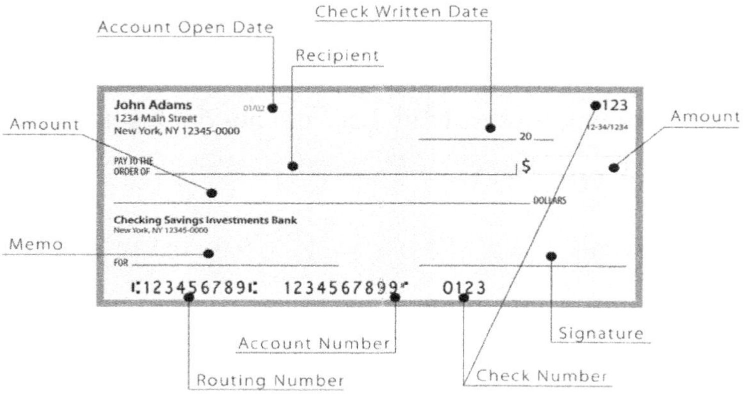

Figure 4-©John T. Takai/Shutterstock

Many bank accounts have attached monthly fees. When opening an account, read the fine print on the paperwork for each type of account and ask questions of the bank personnel before opening an account. Be careful of overdraft fees. Overdraft fees occur when one spends more money than is in their bank account. Credit unions usually have fewer fees and are very user-friendly. There are many types of personal bank accounts. They are:

1. Savings accounts
2. Checking accounts
3. Money market accounts

4. IRAs (investment retirement accounts)
5. Certificates of deposits (CDs)
6. Brokerage accounts (stocks and bonds)

Many people bank online, which is secure if you use secure websites and Wi-Fi. Be careful of public Wi-Fi, because most are not secure and safe. My eighty-seven-year-old mother likes to go into the neighborhood bank branch office and do business and have conversations with the bank tellers. The truth be told, I love to go into the credit union branch and my neighborhood bank branch as well. When I came back from my Icelandic vacation, my favorite teller wanted to see my pictures. I showed them to her until another customer appeared for business.

Banking transactions can also be handled via the drive-thru, on the phone, and online. Remember to check all of your financial accounts monthly. Sometimes inaccurate and fraudulent fees and transactions, along with other unapproved items appear on the account statement. Read the monthly paper and/or online statements for all bank accounts. There are a few additional line items in the budget that must be discussed.

Plan Your Gifts for the Future

The calendar is set and has been set for hundreds of years. The same holidays and special days occur each year. Birthdays, national, federal, and cultural holidays, and anniversary dates never really change. There are annual gift-bearing dates and holidays. The only gift giving dates that often change are graduations, weddings, and baby and wedding showers. However, these dates do not usually occur at the last minute.

As soon as a family member or friend gets engaged, contemplate the gift for their wedding and/or shower gifts. It's already in the budget. If a family friend or relative is in their last year of high school, college, or professional studies, start planning for their graduation gift as soon as possible. It's already in the budget.

There are other gifts to be purchased. Let's be clear, everyone in your circle of family and friends does not need a gift. Look at your yearly calendar to determine the recipients of your gift-giving generosity. These persons can change from year to year. In making life adult choices, one must plan! However, there is one gift-giving day that you cannot forget—Mother's Day! Do this first!

Since re-occurring gift-giving dates occur at the same time each year, purchase gifts for others all year long before the event. Sales and clearances occur in major department stores and online all year long. Research! Make a list and check it twice! I have eleven nieces and nephews. I buy their Christmas and birthday gifts throughout the year. Store the gifts in a sealed container. Do not forget to hide the container just in case a nosey family member happens to find the treasure chest of gifts.

Gifts can also be made with loving care and/or services that can be rendered to family and friends instead of purchasing gifts. Do-It-Yourself (DIY) projects for making homemade gifts can be found in magazines, books, and websites.

Examples of homemade gifts:

1. Vanilla Extract
2. Baked goods
3. Bath salts/scrubs
4. Jewelry
5. Candles
6. Potpourri
7. Butter blends
8. Spice blends
9. Pancake Mix
10. Granola
11. Knitted or crocheted scarf, hat, and mittens

Gift-giving is a budget line item in the wants section of the budget. Planning takes discipline, research, and common sense. Valentine's Day, Black Friday, Christmas, Hanukah, and Kwanza are coming. They come every year and never are canceled. Let's spend and buy everyone a gift! Absolutely not! Only purchase gifts if you can afford to purchase them from the budget.

Create a yearly gift-giving list, designate the amount for each person, and plan accordingly. Before the events, budget and start saving for holidays, birthdays, graduations, showers, and weddings. Plan for Christmas in a separate category. Combine the total Christmas giving amounts and other gift amounts and divide by 12. Save that amount each month for gift-giving time throughout the year.

Gift-giving budgets for each stage of life are present in the Life Budget section. Each year your gift recipients may change, your finances may vary, and additional gift-giving occasions may occur. Wedding and baby showers, just because, housewarmings, and the birth of a baby are other gift-giving events. Nieces, nephews, cousins, aunts, uncles, stepfamily members, godchildren, co-workers, boss, supervisor, barber, and hairdresser are additional gift recipients that could be on the gift recipient list. For exchanging gifts during Christmas and the December holidays, consider giving one family gift, do a Secret Santa gift exchange, or pool monies together as a family and give to a charity, non-profit, or orphanage.

Can you afford to purchase the gifts on your gift list? Please do not enter into debt to buy gifts for others. People in debt cannot afford to purchase lavish gifts at gift-giving time. Be an adult and explain this to family and friends. If necessary, modify and adjust the list of gift recipients and gift amounts. Please do not go into debt or more debt to keep up with and impress others. In past generations, we called "Keeping up with the Joneses." Today's generation is trying to keep up with Kardashians or other lifestyles of reality television personalities. Buy what is affordable.

There is recently a new marketing strategy. It is called Black Friday in July. Many stores have super sales in July, as if

Black Friday in November was not enough. If the budgeted funds are in the account, take advantage of the sales.

Businesses and banks exist to make money, and that money happens to be in your pocket. Businesses and banks advertise everywhere—on billboards, at the gas tank, on the bathroom door stalls in buildings, online, telemarketers, U.S. postal mail, emails, and person to person.

Additional Spending

Be careful of online and casino gambling, daily coffee trips, alcohol, cigarettes, tobacco, and lottery ticket purchases. If these activities and purchases are a part of your lifestyle, budget for them in the monthly budget. For my love of great coffee, I purchased a Nespresso coffee machine with a milk frother. For some people, my coffee machine would not meet their coffee experience, but it satisfies me.

Budget Challenges

No budget will always be perfect. Losing jobs, strikes, job furloughs, and extreme emergencies can affect the budget. Adjust your monthly budget when necessary. Occasionally, monies from the entertainment and/or the allowance category may have to be placed elsewhere in the budget if another budget category is lacking in funds.

CHAPTER 5

Let's Eat

N o matter if you are young, middle aged, a senior citizen, single, married, or divorced, how will you eat? There is no maid, chef, or mother at your apartment to fix meals. What is a person to do? Traditionally, mothers taught their children how to cook and sew at home, and home economic (home ec.) teachers in school taught cooking and sewing to middle school students. The home ec. class has been taken out of many schools. While teaching, I literally remember the day the kitchens were dismantled and the sewing machines were taken out of the home economics classroom in my school. Our students experienced a sad day in their schooling.

A Food Plan

Just in case the Freshman 15 (extra weight from the first year of college), has not left your body, maybe in part due to too many visits to fast-food places, reckless abandon while eating, or lack of food portion control, consider changing your eating habits and making a lifestyle change.

My daughter (the doctor) and son (the health guru) have encouraged me on numerous occasions to change my food habits and live a new, healthy lifestyle. Finally, I heeded their encouragement along with my primary doctor and made some changes. I reduced my food portions, stopped eating flour and sugar, exercised more, stopped eating after 7:00PM, and before 8:45AM, and I lost 82.5 pounds. For the first time in 30 years, I weigh less than 200 pounds.

I've been on many diet plans, and they have worked temporarily, but I always gained the weight back with additional pounds. But then I read and heard about the latest research. The body naturally wants to replenish the fat cells that have shrunk. These cravings intensified after I lost 65 pounds. Oh, the struggle.

The newest eating strategy is intermittent fasting. This method allows the body to rest from food for a long time period. My fasting period is 7:00 PM to 10:00 AM the next morning. This works! Portion control, staying away from fried foods (using an air fryer helps), not eating the skin from poultry, and eating at least two servings of fruits and lots of non-starchy vegetables, and drinking lots of water is working. I fell off the wagon here and there, but intermittent fasting works. Always check with your doctor before trying a new food plan, diet, food lifestyle, and exercise regimen. This is not a diet, but a lifestyle change.

Cooking

These days, there are so many options for not cooking at home. It is very easy to purchase food at fast-food places for all your meals (breakfast, lunch, and dinner), but is it healthy, and does it fit in the budget? Car services pick up food and meals from restaurants and fast-food places and bring them straight to your home. However, homemade food and cooking at home is still the best option for living a healthy lifestyle.

As an adult, make the right choices to eat healthy. These choices do not mean you have to be a gourmet cook or even a decent at-home cook, either. For one, fast-food places should not be visited three times a day. Although some people eat breakfast at their favorite coffee place, lunches at a hamburger joint, and dinner at a pizza place, make sure to cook at home at least three times a week. Homemade is best! Get help and suggestions from your parents, grandparents, family friends, or co-workers on all types of recipes. The internet has a plethora of websites with quick, easy, and healthy ideas and recipes, along with their accompanying cooking techniques.

Another option is your neighborhood supermarket's prepared food section. Whole Foods, Wegmans, Acme, Publix, and many other supermarkets have a prepared food section of hot and cold foods for purchase. A cooked meal can be created and packaged on the spot with all your favorite foods. Many restaurants also have takeout. The latest trend is ordering food via your favorite restaurant, and a car service such as Grubhub, Caviar, or Uber Eats picks up the food and delivers it to your home or office.

Another trend is full meal subscription boxes. Full meal subscription boxes are boxes of food that include pre-measured fresh ingredients, including spices, with recipes attached to a menu that are delivered to your doorstep every week. Each recipe has step-by-step instructions for your delicious, home-cooked, healthy meal. With the help of chefs, companies design meals, complete all of the shopping, and deliver the box of food to your house or apartment. Some customer reviews state the recipes are easy and simple. Amazon.com, via Whole Foods, has meal kits available without a subscription plan.

Supermarkets will also shop from the consumer's food-shopping list and deliver food items to their homes for a nominal fee. Plan meals, make a list of necessary items, order, and pay online. (There are apps to help with this.) Other supermarkets will gather food items from an e-mailed list and have it ready for pick up. Fully seasoned and prepped fresh oven-ready meals packaged in an oven pan and ready for the oven also can be found in supermarkets.

Ready-to-cook meals can be prepared in the slow cooker, Instant Pot, AirFyer, or conventional home ovens. Purchasing ready-to-eat rotisserie chickens is a great way to have a low-cost, healthy meal. Tomorrow's lunch could be tonight's leftovers.

Money Tip

An Inexpensive Healthy Meal
A Rotisserie chicken $5.99
Garden Salad in a bag $3.99
Brown/White Rice Cooked in Bag $1.99

Some television shows give house tours of the rich and famous. The kitchens are usually a gourmet kitchen with state-of-the-art design and appliances, also known as a chef's kitchen. When the refrigerator door is opened in these houses, some celebrities only have Cristal, Gatorade, soda, and water neatly stacked in rows. I hardly see any food present. How do they eat? I guess they eat out, have a personal chef, or have meals delivered each day. Unfortunately, this practice is not just for the rich and famous. Many people have these same practices, but it is a costly one. Everyone should know how to cook at least three basic meals.

Please do not go to your mom's house every day to eat a meal (or meals) as an option not to cook and/or to save money. Adulting is being responsible to cook your meals or purchase food to eat. Stay away from heavily processed foods, because many of those foods have bad fats, high salt content, lots of sugar, unrecognizable and difficult to pronounce ingredients, and lots of calories. With that said, let's add fresh, vibrant, healthy food to your refrigerator and cook some meals at home. Remember to stay away from costly, high in salt and fat pre-packaged and heavily processed bags of food. Keep your kitchen stocked with the following items:

The Refrigerator

Milk	Butter or margarine
Eggs	Mayonnaise
Yogurt	Cheese
Water	Fruits (3 types)
Orange Juice	Cranberry Juice
Apple Sauce	Salad dressings
A loaf of bread	Condiments
Tomatoes	Favorite fresh vegetables

Lettuce (Not iceberg, which has no nutritional value)

The Pantry

Peanut butter	Jelly or preserves of choice
Raisins	Oatmeal (quick or original)
Breakfast cereals	Olive oil
Soups	Tuna fish (packets or cans)
Dried Pasta	Tomato Sauce
Sugar	Flour
Vinegar	Canned vegetables
Coffee and tea	Nuts (all types)

Bread crumbs	Beans and lentils
Rice	Tea

Your breakfast choices should be free of heavy, sugar-laden cereals. Great breakfast cereal choices are Corn Flakes, Raisin Bran, Shredded Wheat, and Cheerios, to name a few. Name brands are mentioned, but there is nothing wrong with store brands or other not-so-familiar brands. Iceberg lettuce is pretty and very affordable, but it does not have any nutritional value. Romaine, Bibb, Boston, and spring mix are better choices, with more nutritional value. Romaine lettuce has the highest nutritional value.

Your freezer should have the following items:

The Freezer

> Two chicken breasts in separate pouches
> Three frozen hamburger patties (made by you or made by the store)
> Two-pound bag of shrimp
> One bag of six 4-ounce salmon filets
> Frozen bags of vegetables of your choice
> Two steaks – your favorite type
> One carton of ice cream (for guilty pleasures)

If your refrigerator's freezer is too small, reduce some of the above quantities. Vegetarians, adjust the above items to your liking.

You need to have a monthly food budget that needs to be followed. Further break the budget down into a weekly food budget, and then a daily food budget. For example, let's use a monthly food budget of $300.00. A weekly food budget would be $75.00, and our daily food budget would be about $10.50. This seems impossible, but it is very doable. Many of items can be used for the entire week, i.e., eggs, milk, bread, oatmeal, and cereal. Each item has many servings.

A serving is a measuring unit of food. (Mathematics will always be a part of your life.) Food labels on packaged foods list the number of servings inside the package. Check the food label for the number of servings. Knowing the number of servings and the calorie count will hopefully limit overeating. A portion is the amount of food on your plate. Portion control is a challenge for many people, especially me. Large portions of meat and carbohydrates lead to gaining weight.

According to the United States recommended food pyramid, there are six food groups. Dairy, grain, protein, vegetables, and fruits, grains, and fats (oils). Desserts need not be a must at every meal. Vegetables should be the largest portions of the plate, and protein and fruits should be the smallest portions of the plate. Please refer to the government's plan on a healthy plate, which can be found at choosemyplate.gov.

Try to plan meals around sale items in the supermarket. If chicken is on sale this week, plan on making multiple chicken dishes. One major supermarket in my neighborhood has chicken breast and chuck ground beef on sale for $2.99 every Tuesday. Many consumers partake of this great sale on Tuesdays. What a savings!

Now stock the refrigerator with the foods of your choice. Always go into the supermarket with a written plan and a budget. Never go to the supermarket hungry. I am guilty of this. When I do, I overspend and my budget goes out of the window. Your mind and stomach will have you purchasing additional foods, not on the list.

What's for dinner? It's late and there are no plans for dinner? If time is a factor, plan to cook the weekly menu dishes on the weekends. Pre-made meals will place meals quickly on the table. Conquer the dinner meal problem with a plan.

There are several ways to plan your meals for the week:

> 1. Plan and write your meals on a calendar or meal planner.
> 2. Choose favorite meals that are easily cooked.
> 3. Choose proteins, vegetables, and fruit that are on sale. Use the supermarket sale circular, internet, and supermarket websites for sales and coupons.

> Healthy eating is about the joy of taste-and the joy of knowing that the investment you just made in your meal will pay dividends, today, tomorrow, and decades from now.[15]

---

[15] Roizen, Michael F. and Crupian, Michael. "*What to Eat When*." (Washington, DC. 2018), 18.

Before cooking, place all of the ingredients and equipment for the meal on the counter. The French term for this process is called *mise en place*. While preparing food and during the cooking process, never use the same utensils and cooking boards while working with raw meat and cooked food. When working with raw meat, wash your hands when done. Then prepare the raw or cooked foods. Cross-contamination can cause food poisoning. Keep the utensils separate, and wipe down the kitchen counter clean with soap.

My favorite kitchen utensils and appliances are my Vitamix, George Foreman grill, Cuisinart Air Fryer, Breville slow cooker, Instant Pot, and a set of sharp Calphalon knives. The Vitamix blends ingredients into smoothies, soups, and ice cream. I grill vegetables and proteins with little or no oil on the George Forman grill or Le Creuset grill pan. I air fry, bake, broil, and toast in the Cuisinart Air Fryer. My Instant Pot quickly cooks brown rice and collard greens. Beans, short ribs, and other dishes cook in the Breville slow cooker. I also have a set of Le Creuset cast iron cookware and All-Clad frying pans. Purchase quality cookware, but purchase what you can afford. Buy a piece at a time. Cheap cookware can possibly give poor results.

Plan a set of meals for one week. Use the free store circular from your favorite supermarket or visit their website as a resource planning guide.

A Sample Day's Menu

Breakfast

1 cup of oatmeal   2 eggs
1 piece of toast (optional)   1 cup of orange juice or orange

Lunch

1 Roast beef and Cheese Sandwich
   2 slices of bread   2 slices of Provolone cheese
   1/4 pound of Roast Beef   Lettuce and tomato
Tossed green salad   2 Tbsp. salad dressing
      1   Apple

Dinner

One 4-6 ounce portion of grilled or baked chicken breast
1/2 cup of cooked brown rice   1 cup of cooked spinach
Tossed green salad   2 Tbsp. of dressing
Dessert (optional)

Exercise #5: Meal Planning
(Breakfast, lunch, and dinner)

Purpose – to create a menu plan for one day of meals and
calculate the cost of the three meals.

Breakfast

Food Item _____   cost $_____

Food Item _____   cost $_____

Food Item _____   cost $_____

Food Item _____   cost $_____

Today's cost for breakfast.   **$_____**

Lunch

Food Item _____   cost $_____

Food Item _____   cost $_____

Food Item _____   cost $_____

105

Food Item _____ cost $_____

Today's cost for lunch. $_____

Dinner
Food Item _____ cost $_____
Food Item _____ cost $_____
Food Item _____ cost $_____
Food Item _____ cost $_____

Today's cost for dinner. $_____
Today's cost for all three meals. $_____

Let's cook easy and healthy meals at home.

Easy Recipes

It's great to have easy, go-to recipes that encourage healthy eating. Below are five easy recipes to assist with cooking in the kitchen. Consult cookbooks, family members, cooking television shows, YouTube videos, and the internet for additional easy how-to recipes. Three of my favorite cookbooks are *The Joy of Cooking, by Irma S. Rombauer, The Silver Palate,* by Sheila Lukins and Julee Russo, and *The Complete American's Test Kitchen TV Show 2001-2018.* Enjoy my favorite designed recipes.

My Food Tips
1. Before placing the protein in the pan, make sure the pan is hot.
2. Do not crowd the proteins in a pan.
3. Less is more. Add seasoning to taste.
4. Clean up as you cook.
5. Use a slow cooker for dinner meals while at work.

My Easy Omelet

Ingredients
3 large eggs
Pan oil spray to coat frying pan
Choice of fillings – cheese, spinach, onions, mushrooms,
green peppers, and/or tomatoes

Directions
1. Heat frying pan on low-medium heat.
2. With a fork, crack the eggs into a bowl. (When breaking
the eggs, be careful of eggshells.)
3. Wisk or beast eggs in a circular motion.
4. Gently pour eggs into the pan.
5. Let eggs cook for 2 minutes.
5. Add the fillings on half of the omelet.
6. Cook for another 1-2 minutes.
7. With a spatula, fold the omelet in half.
8. Cook for another 2 minutes.
9. Gently turn the omelet over and cook another 2 minutes.
Please note: Make sure the egg mixture is cooked all the
way through.

Stir Fry

Ingredients
1 frozen bag or fresh carton of mixed vegetables of
onions, carrots, celery, and broccoli
2 pieces of chicken breast (about 1 lb.)
2 Tbsp. soy sauce
3 Tbsp. Canola or peanut oil
1/2 cup of peanuts or cashews (optional)

Directions

1. Cut vegetables into bite size pieces.
2. Heat frying pan for 3 minutes on medium-high.
3. Pour 3 tablespoons of oil into the pan.
4. When the pan is hot (about 3 minutes), gently lay the chicken into the pan.
5. Do not touch chicken for 3 minutes. Cook chicken until pale and firm.
6. Turn the chicken over and cook chicken for another 3 minutes. Remove chicken to a plate.
7. Add vegetables to the pan. (Do not wipe clean.)
8. Cook for 6 minutes or until desired texture. (Crunchy or soft. Your preference!)
9. Add soy sauce and stir the ingredients.
10. Cut cooked chicken into cubes and place into pan with vegetables.
11. Stir for 3 more minutes and let the flavors join together.
12. Add peanuts or cashews if desired.
13. Remove pan from the stove.

If desired, substitute 1 lb. of shrimp or 1 lb. cubed beef for the chicken. Shrimp will take about 2 minutes to cook and the beef will take about 7 minutes to cook.

If desired, add 2 cups of cooked rice to stir-fry and/or ½ cup of peanuts or cashews.

If desired, put the rice on the plate and add the stir-fry mixture on top of cooked rice.

(Before serving, cut chicken in the middle to make sure there is no pink inside! Pink means the chicken is raw and needs additional cooking time.)

Marlene's Chicken Fingers

Ingredients
1-1b chicken breasts - cut into strips
(or purchase fresh chicken strips or frozen chicken strips)
2 medium eggs
1-cup all-purpose flour
½ cup Canola or peanut oil
1 tsp. salt
1 tsp. pepper

Directions
1. Cut chicken into strips.
2. With a fork, crack the 2 eggs into a bowl. (When breaking the eggs, be careful of eggshells.)
3. Whisk or beat eggs in a circular motion.
4. Combine flour, salt, and pepper into another bowl.
5. With tongs or a fork, place the chicken into the egg mixture (egg wash).
6. Cover chicken in egg wash/mixture.
7. With tongs or a fork, place each strip into the seasoned flour.
8. Heat frying pan on medium heat.
9. When the pan is hot, pour in ½ cup of oil.
10. Shake the excess flour off of the chicken strip.
11. Then gently place 6 chicken strips into the pan.
12. Cook for 4 minutes then turn chicken over with tongs or fork.
13. Cook for another 4 minutes.
14. Place chicken on a paper towel to drain oil.

Place your favorite condiment on the chicken fingers and enjoy it!

Condiments – honey mustard, BBQ sauce, ketchup

Alternative #1
A healthy version of the above is with an air fryer.

Air Fryer Method
Complete steps 1- 4.
5. Spray the air fryer basket with olive oil or a non-stick agent.
6. Place the breaded strips into an air fryer basket.
7. Chicken strips should not touch eat other.
8. Air fry for 10-12 minutes on 300 - 350 degrees.
9. Dip chicken fingers into your favorite condiments and enjoy! (Cut the chicken in the middle to make sure there is no pink inside! Pink means the chicken is raw and needs additional cooking time.)

Alternative #2
Toaster Oven or Conventional Oven
For those without an air fryer, do steps 1- 4
5. Place the strips into a toaster oven or conventional oven at 350 degrees for 25 minutes.
6. Place chicken on a paper towel to drain oil.
7. Place your favorite condiment on the chicken fingers and enjoy it!
(Cut chicken in the middle to make sure there is no pink! Pink means the chicken is raw and needs additional cooking time.)

You Name It Homemade Pizza

Ingredients
Dough
>   3 cups of all-purpose flour
>   2 Tablespoons Canola oil
>   1 Tablespoon of sugar (optional)
>   1 Teaspoon of salt
>   1 packet of active dry yeast.
>   1 cup of warm water
>   2 Tbs. extra virgin olive oil

Toppings

½ Cup pizza sauce or spaghetti sauce

1 Cup of shredded mozzarella or a blend of your favorite cheeses

Any toppings of choice (pepperoni, mushrooms, onions, broccoli, pork or turkey sausage, etc.)

Directions for Dough

1. Pour the contents of one packet of yeast into 1 cup of warm water.
2. Stir to combine and let it sit until it bubbles or foams.
3. Mix all of the ingredients except the yeast and water.
4. Then pour the yeast mixture into the flour mixture.
5. Stir with a wooden spoon or use a mixer to incorporate all the ingredients.
6. Knead the dough by hand on smooth surface or use the kneading attachment on the mixer.
7. Place dough in a bowl and cover with plastic wrap.
8. Let dough rise for 2 - 3 hours. (Dough should double in size.)

Please note: This can be done the day before or on the weekend. The dough freezes well in a sealed plastic bag.

Directions for Pizza

1. Preheat oven to 450 degrees.
2. Put 1 Tbsp. of Canola oil in a pan (preferably cast-iron);
3. Roll out the dough with a rolling pin or stretch and flatten the dough with your fingertips to the edge of the pan.
4. With a spoon, spread the tomato sauce in a circular motion.
5. Sprinkle shredded mozzarella and other cheeses over the pie.
6. Sprinkle the toppings over the sauce.
7. Drizzle 2 Tbsp. of extra olive oil on top of the pizza pie.
8. Place in the oven for 8-10 minutes.

Alternative #1 –
Buy pre-made pizza dough from the supermarket.

Alternative #2
If you suffer from digestive problems (reflux) from acidic foods like tomatoes, omit the sauce and only use cheeses.

Please note: If the dough is ready, the above pizza will be complete and ready for consumption in less than the time it takes to call for pizza delivery.

MJC Mouth-Watering Steak

Ingredients
2 - 8oz New York Strip or Bone-in Rib Eye (room temperature)
2 Tbsp. unsalted butter
1 Tsp. salt and 1 Tsp. pepper
2 sprigs of fresh rosemary and/or thyme
3 Tbsp. Canola oil

Directions

1. Heat a cast-iron pan for 3 minutes on medium-high. Make sure the pan is hot.
2. Salt and pepper the steak on both sides.
3. Pour 3 Tbsp. of olive oil into the pan and heat for 3 minutes.
4. When the pan is hot, gently lay the steak into the pan.
5. Cook steak for 4 minutes (Do not touch the steak.)
6. After 4 minutes, with tongs, turn the steak over.
7. Add butter and rosemary and/or thyme to the pan.
8. Baste the steak with butter. (Spoon the butter over the steak.)
9. After cooking both sides of the steak, remove it from pan. Place the steak on a plate and cover for five minutes to let the steak rest. (If the steak is not allowed to rest, the juices of steak will bleed out when sliced.)

Coupons

Manufacturers and supermarkets offer coupons to the consumer by reducing the cost of a product with money off coupons. This marketing tool gets the consumers' attention, advertises a product, buys loyalty, gets repeat business, and targets consumers.[16] The consumer saves money. Coupons often have restrictions. There are specifications on the size(s) of the product and how many items must be purchased. Carefully read the coupon and especially look for the expiration date, if any. Coupons help reduce food costs. For additional savings for the consumer, some supermarkets double and triple the amount of the coupons with a limit.

Three types of coupons:
1. Manufacturer's coupon – from a specific company of the given product
2. Store Coupon – the store sponsors the coupon
3. Internet coupon – coupons can be found on the internet from various websites

Apply for a store loyalty card and keep the mini card on your key ring for extra savings at the cash register or use the store app for savings. In some stores that use the loyalty card, it must be scanned to receive the savings, and other stores allow

---

[16] Fontinelle, Amy. "Why Do Companies Print Coupons?" Updated Jun 25, 2019. Accessed April 20, 2020. https://www.investopedia.com/financial-edge/0911/why-do-companies-print-coupons.aspx.

the input of the customer's phone number that was used to set up the store account into the kiosk. Some supermarkets give everyone the store discount savings on certain products without a store saving card. Know your supermarket!

Understanding Food Labels

For the consumer to make informed decisions about a product, the food label lists the nutritional facts, calories, and serving size. When shopping in the food market, compare products based on the information listed on the food label. For example, the same product from different companies may have huge differences in sodium amounts.

Supermarket Shopping Tips

Never go into the supermarket hungry. Hunger pains break down the resolve to purchase healthy foods, plus the hunger pains assist in buying unnecessary foods. Food companies pay additional fees to supermarkets to place their product at the beginning and end of aisles or at eye level in the aisle. Price check and read food labels to compare similar food items. Shop with a personal food list from a prepared set of weekly food menus. More often than not, each shopper goes in the supermarket for specific items and comes out with a whole lot more. Be familiar with your favorite supermarket, which will help you move more quickly through the market. To save money, purchase fresh vegetables and fruits in season and foods on sale. Budget for food purchases. This concept is difficult for me because I often go over my price range while in the supermarket. Quality food is my passion!

Using food shopping apps on the phone can help shoppers stay on budget. Also, check the unit price per food item. By law, food labels are on food products, and this information allows the consumer to be knowledgeable about a food item's servings, nutrition, nutrients, and ingredients.

Although I have never used this process of shopping, there are electronic devices that allow the consumer to scan and bag each item as they shop, track spending, and pay the total costs to the cashier at the end of the shopping experience. One of my walking buddies uses this type of technology while food shopping. She states that process saves time and gives an accurate account of the costs during the shopping experience.

Fast-food Restaurants

If you must, fast-food restaurant eating is an option. Nevertheless, many of fast-food choices are not always the healthiest of choices. Some fast-food restaurants have salads and grilled chicken. Is the average person going to eat a salad at lunch with low-fat dressing, and for dinner eat grilled chicken with no French fries at their favorite fast-food place?

There will be times when a fast-food restaurant is the only option. I visit these restaurants on road trips. Try to select the healthiest food choices while visiting fast-food restaurants. First, many fast-food restaurants' menu selections contain high amounts of fat and salt. Everyone should limit their fat and salt intake. The United States Department of Health and Human Services (HHS) recommends 20-35 grams of fat per day. Do not use all your allowable grams of fat at one meal. Some fast-food restaurants list the calories of each food item on the menu screen next to the food item, and other restaurants list calories and nutritional information on their websites, posters, and in printed booklet form. Apps like *Cheap Day* list the nutritional value for over 750 fast-food restaurants.

Each fast-food restaurant must post or have available the nutrition values of each item they sell. There are several books you can purchase that list the nutrition values of each food item from many of your favorite fast-food restaurants. The above information is listed online as well. Be careful of salad dressings. Many salad dressings have lots of sugar, fat, and high caloric amounts. Read the labels!

Fast-food and restaurant eating costs must be included in your food budget. These costs should not be more than your grocery bills.

Be careful of sugary drinks, i.e., sodas, lattes with sugar, lemonades, and ice teas. Drink plenty of water! Plain water has no calories. Add lemon or lime slices or cucumbers to flavor the water. Many sugary drinks and alcoholic beverages have loads of empty calories. Our bodies request and need 6-8 glasses of water each day for healthy living.

Etiquette

Etiquette is a set of acceptable rules for behavior or code of behavior in a public setting. There are rules of etiquette for table manners, business, and everyday life. As a school writing assignment at the age of sixteen, George Washington copied *110 Rules of Civility & Decent Behavior in Company and Conversation* written by French Jesuits in 1595. Many of these rules are outdated, but many are still applicable today. My favorite rule is #1- "Every action done in company, ought to be with some sign of respect, to those that are present."[17]

Table Etiquette

1. Arrive on time to food events.
2. Eat with your mouth closed.
3. Place the napkin on your lap after sitting down.
4. Applying lipstick should never happen at the table.
5. Technology should not be used at the table. Excuse yourself and leave the table if a phone call must be answered or made.
6. Comb or brush your hair in the bathroom, not at the table.
7. Men are to stand when a woman leaves and arrives at the

[17] Foundation Magazine. *"George Washington's Rules of Civility & Decent Behavior in Company and Conversation"*, n.d., accessed September 10, 2020. http://www.foundationsmag.com/civility.html.

dining table. (This is hardly done anymore.)

8. Everyone waits to eat until all are served.
9. When finished eating, place fork and knife on top of your plate to signify completion.
10. Elbows should never rest on the table.

There are additional etiquette table manners, but I highly recommend the above ten.

Table Settings

There is an established table setting for casual and formal dining. Some people sit at the table and do not know which eating utensils to use. An everyday table setting has the fork to the left of the plate on top of a napkin. The knife is to the right of the plate with the spoon to the right of the knife. The salad plate goes on top of the dinner plate and the soup bowl goes on top of the salad plate. The water and wine glasses go to the right of the plate.

Figure 5-©New Africa/Adobe Stock

For formal dining, there are additional eating utensils on the table—salad and dinner forks, soup and dessert spoons, dinner and bread knives, and three glasses, water, white wine, and red wine glasses. A bread plate is also included in formal dining. The salad fork is on the outside, and then the dinner fork.

118

Remember, the dinner fork is the largest fork and closest to the dinner plate. One of my favorite scenes in the movie *Pretty Women* is when the character Vivian asks Barney, the hotel manager, for a dinner etiquette lesson. She was to accompany Edward, to a very important business dinner meeting at a very expensive restaurant and did not want to embarrass him for her lack of knowledge on using the correct eating utensil at the appropriate time.

Tipping at Restaurants

Tipping is customary for an enjoyable dining experience. Tips supplement the salaries of the servers, waitresses, and waiters. It is customary to tip 18–22% of the bill to the server at the restaurant. If a sommelier serves wine, tip 18–22% of the wine bill.

Most restaurants show suggested tip amounts at the bottom of the bill. However, most people tip on the total amount of the bill, which includes the tax. For parties of six or more, some restaurants include the tip within the total. Carefully read the bill. Some diners tip twice without realizing the bill included the tip because of the large party.

Exercise

One way to keep your body healthy is to exercise. Consult a doctor before taking on different types of exercise. The gym offers equipment to complete cardio, toning, and strengthening exercises. There are all types of gyms with various types of affordable and luxury memberships. Exercise at least 30 minutes three to five times a week. Exercise classes are also on YouTube and websites.

Walk with friends, go to the gym, exercise at the neighborhood playground, exercise at local churches and gyms that offer Zumba classes, line dancing, and boot camp for a nominal fee. Some companies have a workout room. I believe that walking five days a week for at least 30 minutes is one of the easiest, doable, and least expensive exercises to do daily. There are many options. Be careful not to over-exercise, which can cause injuries.

Walking, playing tennis, swimming, and indoor cycling are my exercises of choice. I am grateful to my Proverbs 31 Enon Tabernacle Baptist Church Walking Buddies who walk with me five to six days a week each morning. We encourage each other with our daily food intake and exercise.

Take good care of your body, because you only have one life to live. Eat right, exercise daily, sleep at least eight hours a night, and have annual doctor visits. Guaranteed health is given to no one, but the above s will help you maintain a great healthy body. There are benchmark doctor checkups/screenings for every age group. Ask your doctor for a timeline and their recommendations for screenings.

One major lesson I learned later in life is that exercise is great, but the monitoring of measured food portions is key. Although I used to exercise a great deal, I also ate volumes of food. Diet is 80 percent of food consumed and exercise is 20 percent.[18] Today, I exercise five to seven days a week for one hour and consistently weigh and measure my food. (I have been known to cheat on occasion.) A healthy diet and healthy finances are crucial to having a great life.

Wisely choose the company you keep. I quote both Euripides and the early Greek poet Menander as saying, "Bad company corrupts good character."[19] Your friends say a lot about who you are. Stay true to who you are and do not change who you are for a friend. A friend will lift you, encourage, be loyal, a good listener, a confidant, be truthful, comfort you in troubled times, and rejoice with you in good times. Some friends are seasonal and are here only for a short time period. Know when to move on, and be careful of the company you keep.

---

[18] Edwards, Terri. "Healthy Weight Loss = 80% Nutrition + 20% Exercise", n.d., Accessed April 15, 2020. https://nutritionstudies.org/healthy-weight-loss-80-nutrition-20-exercise/.

[19] Ling, P. H. "A Quotation from Euripides." *The Classical Quarterly*, vol. 19, no. 1, 1925, pp. 22–27. *JSTOR*, www.jstor.org/stable/635953. Accessed 12 Nov. 2020.

Know why your friend is in your life and when to leave the friendship. Finally, a good friend shows himself friendly.

Part III

Life Budgets

CHAPTER 6

The Single Life

Congratulations. Welcome to adulthood. Adulting is your life now, and you get to make decisions for your life. Adulting happens every minute of the day. You may want to take a break from adulting, but you are now leading and guiding the direction of your life. Unfortunately, not wanting to adult on a particular day is not an option.

Singleness is an unmarried state for an individual. In singleness, there is no legal document binding two people together in marriage. Singleness comes with or without children. Some singles choose to adopt children without a spouse. Other single women may choose to have children via in-vitro fertilization without a husband. At the end of this chapter, the single budget will be for singles with or without children. If you have a child or children, please read about raising children and parenting beginning on page 165.

In singleness, one has the freedom to accomplish various aspirations that would be otherwise challenging to do so within a marriage. Embrace this time in your life, and do not stagnate while waiting for Mr. or Mrs. Right. Go to school, continue your education, travel all over the world, start a business, save money, and accomplish career goals without having a spouse affected by your schedule or time. Singleness may be your choice and marriage may not be.

Someone has read your resume, liked it, and gave you an interview. A telephone interview and/or a face-to-face interview are part of the interview process.

Congratulations again! A possible new employer has loved your resume and interviews, and they have offered you a steady job. You have acquired your first real job! Please follow the tips for your new employment, and bear in mind that they are not in any specific order.

Dress for success at your employment and adhere to the dress code of your employer/company. Be punctual to work, leave at the designated time—and not one minute before. Work the contracted hours, and give the employer your best during the entire time you are expected to work.

In the workplace, speak the King's English with proper grammar and no profanity. Personal cell phone use should only occur during breaks and lunchtime. (There are a few exceptions to this.) Be kind and considerate to your boss, co-workers, custodial staff, cafeteria workers, clients, customers, and administrators. Be kind to everyone even if they do not return the kindness. Remain professional at all times. Keep the company's private business to yourself. Insider information should not be spread around to others.

When using the company's phone, start with a greeting, your name, and how can I help you? Know who the CEO is, what they look like, gather information on them, and read some articles or books they have written.

Dating

What is dating? Why date? Is dating necessary to find a mate? What is the purpose of dating? How and where do you find the woman or man of your dreams?

Dating is when two people decide to spend time together doing various activities to decide if they like each other or if they are compatible. Dating is a period of exploration, and it allows two people the opportunity to get to know each other. The dating experience allows a person to decide if they want to spend time with the other person. Before dating, love and spend time with yourself, and get to know who you are before getting to know someone else.

There are computer programs that match people together after a personality profile is taken. The computer, via algorithms, matches people that will complement each other's personality.

Where and what happens on a date? Do I need to date? How long are dates supposed to last, and are blind dates a good idea? Should a date end early if one does not enjoy the other or the date? Is going "Dutch" permissible, or should the man always pay for the date? As the young lady, should I offer to pay? These questions have different answers based on personal viewpoints. Review these questions and formulate a viewpoint.

There are a great many places to go on a date. The movies, museums, nature walks, bowling, roller and/or ice skating, amusement parks, picnics, intramural and professional sports games, restaurants, skiing, church outings, parties, forums on topics of interest, plays, horseback riding, and concerts. Each of these suggestions can be done in a city setting, the suburbs, or in the country.

A date can be as short as an hour or as long as four hours. A short date would be at any coffee shop, an hour nature walk, book reading, or a short picnic.

There is a new philosophy on the length of time of a date. Short dates can give quick information about the other person. If the date is not enjoyable, the short date will not go on forever. Date with a purpose, not for a free meal or excitement.

The purpose of dating is to get to know a person, see if both personalities "gel" together, and see if both parties truly like each other. Some people have a list of the qualities and characteristics that they are looking for in a mate. However, there may be some items on your list that you may have to compromise on. For example, the list may include that your potential partner must have brown hair. However, what happens if your new boyfriend or girlfriend has red hair? Is that a deal-breaker? I believe hair color should not be a deal-breaker, but some people who have those viewpoints. When deciding to date a person, do you have non-negotiable positions about the qualities of your dating partner? Know and have your own standards and value system. A boy- or girlfriend should not go against your value system. Determine what you want and do not want. Know what you will and will not do.

I believe there is nothing wrong with dating multiple people as long as everyone involved knows that this is the situation. When a decision has been made to be in a committed relationship, please respect that commitment. In other words, do not cheat!

Possible Deal Beakers
I will only date:

1. a non-smoker.
2. one who has a high school diploma or a college degree.
3. is of the same religious faith.
4. a drug-free person.
5. a non-alcoholic.
6. one who is kind and not abusive.
7. one who respects his or her parents.
8. someone who is childless.

9. one who is honest.
10. one who is not self-absorbed.

My friend Renee believes in her "Three "C's" concept to dating and marriage. The Three C's are conviction, compromise, and communication.

1. Conviction – Stay true to your belief system in religion, standards, lifestyles, etc.
2. Compromise – Be willing to reciprocally sacrifice for one another.
3. Communication – Share your feelings and be willing to be vulnerable, and be truthful in what you say and do.

For marriage, I would add another "C", and it would be commitment.

The following exercise is not an official scientific dating profile, but a snapshot into the type of person who is dateable in your eyesight.

Exercise #6: Characteristics and Qualities Wanted in a Dating Partner

Write a list of the physical and personal characteristics and qualities wanted in a dating partner.

1. _____   6. _____
2. _____   7. _____
3. _____   8. _____
4. _____   9. _____
5. _____   10. _____

Examples of qualities and characteristics:

Outgoing, religious, non-smoker, drug-free, "buff", skinny, curvy, ambitious, slacker, college-educated, intellectual, nice dresser, pessimistic, trustworthy, driven, optimistic, health nut, sports fanatic, attractive, well-groomed, spiritual, Christian, social drinker, thoughtful, loquacious, naturalist, musical, romantic, patient, adventurous, world traveler, foodie, home cook, trustworthy, techie or tech-savvy, animal lover, confident, humorous, goal-driven, selfish, visionary

Exercise #7: Dating Partner Deal Breakers

List the personal and physical characteristics and quality deal breakers that are unacceptable. List them in the order of importance, with number one being of utmost importance.

1. _____

2. _____

3. _____

4. _____

5. _____

At the beginning of a relationship, look for red flags that are unacceptable. Physical and mental abuse and controlling people are major red flags. Know your standards. Run for your life!

My First Apartment

Our first need in life is housing. This will probably be your largest budget item. Where will you lay your head down at night? Rent an apartment that you can afford to pay monthly without borrowing from others to make up the difference. If you have the monetary means and are responsible, purchasing a home is an option as well. However, being a homeowner carries many responsibilities.

You cannot live with your parents for the rest of your life. Living at home may be a comfortable place for you, but it is time to move out on your own. To acquire a new apartment, savings are needed for the move from your parent's house to an apartment. It is time to move out on your own and lease your first apartment. Before packing, consider the following information:

1. How do I look for a place to live?
2. What is my monthly affordable rent?
3. What area or neighborhood is a great place to live?
4. How many bedrooms and bathrooms do I need?
5. Are the utilities included? (Utilities are gas, water, and electric.)
6. What is the down payment?
7. Are pets allowed?

Is a luxury apartment full of wonderful amenities affordable? Amenities are pleasure items included in the rent,

LIFE 101

i.e., a doorman, valet parking, swimming pool, hot tub, beauty shop, gym/fitness center, community room, and laundry room. Use a Can-I-Afford-It online calculator, which is based on a steady salary and expenses. Spend no more than 25 percent of your take-home income on rent costs. The rent bill belongs to the occupant. I have heard stories of parents paying their adult children's rent each month or supplementing their rent costs.

One's finances dictate what apartment is affordable. Now that you are an adult, make the difficult decisions and choose affordable lodging. Being independent means depending on yourself for your life choices and responsibilities, and being self-sufficient and self-reliant! Therefore, parents should not supplement or be asked to help pay their adult children's monthly rent! Being dependent means depending on your parents/guardians or someone else. The beginning letter of independence is "I".

The monthly rent will be sent or given to the landlord. A landlord is usually the owner or the representative of the owner of the apartment. The landlord/owner decides rental costs and date due. In some states, the landlord can enter an apartment for emergencies and repairs without the renter's permission or presence. Is the landlord the new parent?

Every month, usually on the 1st of the month, the landlord seeks the monthly rent for the occupation of the apartment. Some have a specific amount of days for the grace period. If the

133

rent is late, the owner often accesses a late fee. The monthly rent must be paid, whether you live in the apartment or not. For instance, you still have to pay it if you are traveling abroad, taking a vacation, in the hospital, studying out-of-state, or being a caretaker of a family member elsewhere. If the lease allows subletting, someone else can take over the lease and live in the apartment while the first renter is gone. Carefully read the terms of the lease agreement. Not every lease allows subletting to another individual.

While in medical school, my daughter decided to take a year off and work in Nairobi, Kenya, in West Africa. Her landlord allowed her to leave her belongings and sublet the apartment to another individual during that year. The subletter took over her lease for the year and paid the rent directly to the owner per their agreement while she was out of the country.

The neighborhood, location, square footage, and amenities help determine the monthly rental cost. Typically, $500 - $1,100 a month is an average range of rent for a one-bedroom apartment. (This is not true in California, New York City, or gentrified city living.) If there are roommates, the rent and utilities can be divided, thus lowering the costs. However, roommate living entails each person financially doing their part, cleaning and managing the apartment together, additional bedrooms, and respecting each other's space. Hopefully, this was learned and experienced at home, and in the dorm and apartments while in college.

What town, city, state, and neighborhoods are desired? Are those places affordable? The same type of apartment will have different monthly rental costs due to the location, amenities, newly renovated, older vs. newer, and the appliances of the apartment.

Some apartments include utilities, which are gas, electricity, and water. Some apartments include one, two, all three utilities, or none at all. Carefully read the newspaper or internet advertisements to find out what is or is not included. The inclusion of the utilities will enable you to afford a higher-priced apartment. If the utilities are not included, ask the landlord what the average costs are for water, gas, heat, and electricity. Other apartments may include Wi-Fi and cable.

How many bedrooms are affordable? Single people may only need one or two bedrooms if they do not have children. A roommate can also help with expenses.

Believe it or not, some apartments do not have bedrooms. These living spaces are called studios or efficiencies. In a studio, the living room and bedroom are the same. In this configuration, most people sleep on a futon or a sofa sleeper. What is affordable? Make an educated financial decision on living arrangements. Live within your means. Do not try to impress family and friends with your decision.

The apartment has been found! How much is the down payment? Usually, the landlord wants first and last month's rent in advance, as well as a security deposit. To rent or lease an apartment, many landlords usually require a security down payment before entering a rental agreement. Some landlords may ask for move-in cost fees.

When renting an apartment, there is a lease agreement with the owner or the landlord to live in their place for a given amount of time for a specific monthly cost.

Figure 6-©Wirojsid/Adobe Stock

The agreement can be month to month, a six-month lease, or a yearly lease. Before signing on the line, carefully read the terms of the lease agreement. When the lease agreement is signed, you have entered into a binding legal contract. The agreement is to pay $_____ each month for a specific time period.

If the lease is broken for any reason, a financial penalty may be required for that decision. The landlord has the last month's rent and can require additional monies due them according to the signed lease. The return of the security deposit is based on the signed lease agreement and the discretion of the landlord.

Does the apartment allow pets? Some apartments charge pet rent, and other apartments do not allow pets in their establishments at all. Choose the apartment carefully! Are there any amenities included with the apartment?

The apartment lease has been completed, signed, and approved. Now what? How will the apartment be outfitted? Will Crate and Barrel, Ethan Allen, or Bassett outfit the entire apartment? News flash! Every item in the apartment needs to be purchased with cash. Save and budget for furniture. Do not go into debt purchasing brand new furniture. Other options include friends and family cast-offs, consignment shops, Craigslist, Facebook Marketplace, and thrift shops. Be careful and mindful when going to unknown homes to purchase items. Take someone with you and be careful. Finally, save for dream items and pay cash. This is not an emergency!

Although the apartment is leased and not owned by the renter, rental insurance is needed to protect the renter's valuables inside the apartment. Obtain renters insurance from an insurance company.

Is the monthly rent affordable? You should not spend more than twenty-five percent of your net (after-tax) income on rent/mortgage. For example, a person whose income is $3000.00 per month should have monthly rental fees of no more than $750.00 a month (25% of the take-home pay). For further help, use an online rent affordability calculator.

"Don't keep up with the Joneses!" This is a familiar saying. The Joneses are typically friends, family, neighbors, or even

137

enemies who have what you want, and you will purchase those items at any cost because you do not want those people to have more than you have. Even if you can afford to do so, covetousness and jealousy are wrong motives. Check your motives!

What should I look for when looking for an apartment?

Apartment Checklist

1. Location: Check out the neighborhood in the morning, afternoon, late evening, and the weekend.

2. Rental cost: Lease an affordable apartment.

3. Utilities: Which ones are included or not included, and their costs.

4. Connections: Check for cell phone reception, Wi-Fi, and cable access.

5. Walkthrough: If possible, visit the apartment.

6. Know the amenities: These include swimming pool, fitness room, community center, laundry room, and many more.
7. Commute time: Calculate the distance and travel time to your employment by car or public transportation during rush hour or work hours.

8. Get referrals: Check the reviews from others who have rented at the apartment complex. These reviews can be found online. You can also ask those that you meet while at the apartment complex while on a fact-finding mission.

9. Neighbors: If possible, check out the neighbors. Are they quiet or loud, have lots of kids, loud animals that bark or quiet ones, party-like, etc.?

10. Condition: Make sure everything is in workable condition and complete a thorough check before renting the apartment.

You, the renter, are accountable to the landlord. There are renter's rights. Research and know them; they differ in each state. The landlord has specific responsibilities to renters. If there are any problems or concerns, the landlord, super, or managing agent will be the contact person. Best wishes and good luck. Do not forget to take a picture of your first apartment for your scrapbook, memories, or posterity. Start packing! Let's look for an affordable apartment. Research! Do not go beyond your housing budget limit for the apartment of your dreams.

Remember, if you choose not to renew at the end of the lease agreement, the return of the security deposit is based on the signed agreement and the discretion of the landlord. Schedule a final walkthrough with the landlord. Leave the apartment in good condition, and take pictures upon your final departure.

Exercise #8: Apartment Hunting

Monthly rental payment $_____

Apartment address – _____

Circle the included utilities. <u>Gas Water Electric Heat</u>

Circle the utilities **not** included. <u>Gas Water Electric Heat</u>

Studio ____ Loft ____ Duplex _____ Triplex_____

Bedrooms _____ Bathrooms_____

List the amenities_____

Cable Ready – <u>Yes or No</u>   Free Wi-Fi – <u>Yes or No</u>

Housekeeping

How will this apartment be cleaned? If a housekeeper is not an affordable line item, the occupant of the apartment will clean it. That's you! However, ask family and friends for recommendations on house cleaning products that do the best job. Pick a day to clean the apartment and choose a day to do the laundry. Or do both on the same day. Many people choose to do household chores on the weekend.

Laundry

Never wash all the whites and colored clothes together at the same time. Why? Some colors bleed color in the wash. Have a separate washing cycle for whites, darks, reds, and light-colored clothes. The whites will never be white again when washed with

140

the reds and dark clothing. When pouring bleach into the white clothes' wash cycle, be careful. If you spill bleach, it will ruin anything and everything in its path.

Cleaning

Clean as you go. Daily wipe down the shower stall; clean out the tub after each use. Wash dishes or use the dishwasher. Sweep the floor and mop the floor when dirty.

As soon as you leave the bed in the morning, make the bed when you get out of it. Walking into a bedroom with everything in place gives a calming experience. Clutter, disarray, and chaos weigh heavily on the brain. View the many checklists available online to assist with an organization plan of housekeeping and laundry chores. In Appendix III a household checklist is provided.

There are a percentage of people reading this book who have the monetary funds or who are qualified to purchase a house or condominium (condo) without living in an apartment first. Good for you! Owning a house has many responsibilities. As a homeowner, the responsibilities are great but doable. If something breaks, the homeowner is responsible to fix it. An emergency fund must be in place! If there are funds to purchase a house and the responsibility of homeownership is not a problem, please go to page 170.

Exercise #9: The Single Life Budget
(With or Without Children)

Month-	Estimated	Actual
Income (Net)		
Primary Job		
Part-time Job		
Interest/Investments		
Child Support		
Total Income		
Expenditures – Needs		
Savings/ Emergency Fund		
Retirement Savings		
Tithe/Charity		
Food		
Groceries		
Take out – Restaurants		
Housing		
Rent/Mortgage		
HOA		
Rental/House Insurance		
Utilities		
Water		
Gas/Heat		
Electricity		
Transportation		
Car Note/Public/Rideshare		
Gasoline		
Car Maintenance		
Car Insurance		
Utilities		
Water		
Heat/Gas		
Electricity		
Childcare/Education		

Month-	Estimated	Actual
Health Insurance		
Other-		
Total Needs Expenditures		
Expenditures – Wants		
Clothes		
Dental Insurance		
Life Insurance		
Cell Phone		
Cable TV		
Internet- Wi-Fi		
Student Loans		
Personal Care/Toiletries		
Credit Card #1		
Yearly Gift Giving		
December Holiday/Christmas Gifts		
Pet Care		
Gym Membership		
Hairdresser/Barber		
Vacation		
Allowance		
Subscriptions/Streaming		
Entertainment		
Miscellaneous		
Other -		
Total Want Expenditures		
Total Needs & Wants Expenditures		
Total Money Left		

You are self-reliant, on your own, and in charge of making your own income and good decisions for your life.

Exercise #10: Annual Gifts – Single Life

Budget Amount - $_____

I plan to buy gifts for the following people:

Name	Occasion	Gift	Cost	Date	Purchased
Mom	Birthday				
Dad	Birthday				
Family-	Birthday				
Family-	Birthday				
Family-	Birthday				
Family-	Birthday				
Friend 1	Birthday				
Friend 2	Birthday				
Parents	Anniversary				
	Bridal/Baby Shower				
	Wedding 1				
	Wedding 2				
	Valentine's Day				
	Valentine's Day				
	Graduation				
	Miscellaneous				
	Miscellaneous				
Total					

Exercise #11: December Holiday/Christmas Gift List – Single Life

Budget Amount - $_____

I plan to buy Christmas/Holiday gifts for the following people:

Name	Gift	Cost	Date	Purchased
Mom				
Dad				
Grandparents				
Grandparents				
Family-				
Family-				
Family-				
Family -				
Friend 1				
Friend 2				
Total				

The above gift-giving budget lists must be modified to fit your family structure, circle of friends, lifestyle, and finances. There is no obligation to purchase gifts that you cannot afford.

Are you getting ready to get engaged, and maybe even are planning a wedding? Go to Appendix II–Planning A Wedding

Are you ready to move onto the next stage of life?

CHAPTER 7

The Married Life

You've had your first job for a while and you've dated and had several relationships. Is marriage in the cards for you? Do you want to get married? Let's be clear. Some people do not want to be married. No judgment! The choice of marriage may or may not be your choice or someone else's choice. Everyone will not get married! Some will not find Mr. or Mrs. Right, and others may not be chosen, or they may be unhappy with the choices.

Exercise #12: Choosing a Mate

List the characteristics you both have in common

1. _____   6. _____
2. _____   7. _____
3. _____   8. _____
4. _____   9. _____
5. _____   10. _____

What matters to you most? Rank each of the following in the order of importance, with #1 being the most important and #10 being the least important.

	Me	Future Spouse
Physical Appearance		
Religion		
Income		
Hobbies		
Education		
Race		
Friends		
Size of family		
Introvert/extrovert		
Goal-Oriented		
Physical Attraction		

Exercise #13: Will You Marry Me?

What do I have to offer? What do I bring to the table? List your positive and negative characteristics and qualities. Be honest.

Positive	Negative
1.	1.
2.	2.
3.	3.
4.	4.
5.	5.

Examples of attributes, qualities or characteristics:

Outgoing, religious, non-smoker, non-drug user, "buff", skinny, hard worker, slacker, educated, nice dresser, pessimistic, optimistic, attractive, well-groomed, visionary, sports enthusiast, Christian, social drinker, smart, comical, spiritual, world traveler, home cook/chef, musical, loquacious, shy.

Marriage is not 50/50, but 100/100 percent. Marriage takes work, and both people must subscribe to working together on the marital relationship. Being married is a commitment between two people, and the marriage certificate is signed by them to signify their love and commitment with all the legal rights to becoming husband and wife. The wedding is a manifestation and celebration of the love between two people.

Ask questions before the marriage begins and do not wait until the honeymoon night to find out. Research and know everything possible about your intended spouse before the wedding. Additional information about your spouse will be learned as you experience life together. Marriage is a huge commitment to each other. The wedding is one day, but the marriage is hopefully a lifetime. Plan for your marriage life. Please revisit the Three C's of dating and marriage on page 130.

Are you now ready to make the next big decision in your life? Has Mr. or Mrs. Right been found? Have you found a person you want to live with forever? Can you live with his or her imperfections for a lifetime? Either you want to marry a certain special person, or someone wants to marry you. The decision is...? I believe that I am ready to get married! Are you sure?

Pre-marital Counseling

Being mentally, spiritually, and financially ready for marriage with adequate pre-marital counseling will hopefully help with the success of a great marriage. Before marriage, seek adequate pre-marital counseling from your minister, priest, or marriage counselor to help prepare both you and your partner for a long-lasting healthy marriage. Attend at least eight to ten sessions; one session is not enough! Some couples even go to pre-marital counseling before becoming engaged. Each person should be intentional in finding out if there are childhood wounds that have not been dealt with or addressed. Taking unaddressed childhood wounds into a marriage can be detrimental.

Financial issues and infidelity are two major issues that often occur in marriage. Topics discussed during pre-marital counseling should include finances, parenting styles, housekeeping, core values, and gender roles, blending families, sex, meddling in-laws, and noisy friends to mention a few. Ask the real important questions now! Do not wait until the marriage begins. Unfortunately, pre-marital counseling will not foolproof a marriage, but it will help ask and answer the important tough questions and concerns for a healthy marriage.

Potential Pre-Marital Questions

1. Are children wanted, and if so, how many?
2. Do you subscribe to a budget, and what does it look like?
3. Is there a consistent monthly savings plan?
4. Do you possess cooking and/or household cleaning skills?
5. Is there debt, and if so, how much? What is plan for eradicating this debt?
6. What are your five-year and ten-year goals/plans?
7. What are your beliefs on gender roles?
8. Is religion a part of your life, and if so, how big?
9. Will there be a stay-at-home parent?
10. Will there be joint or separate banking accounts?

Many of these questions can be answered when your relationship becomes monogamous. (Persons who do not want to be monogamous should wait to be married until they are ready to do so.)

In these pre-marital sessions, the counselor, minister, or priest will talk to both parties about their expectations and thoughts on specific topics mentioned above. During these sessions, the couples will discuss, ask, answer, hash out, plan, and re-evaluate. Pre-marital counseling assists you in getting ready for your upcoming marriage. Communication is key! Some couples realize after going through pre-marital counseling that the timing is not right for marriage, or they might even realize that they are not compatible and choose not to marry their intended.

Do not be offended if your fiancé or fiancée asks for a pre-nuptial agreement. A pre-nuptial is a legal document that states what the other marriage partner will receive in property, money, and assets in case of a divorce. Each state has its own set of laws concerning pre-nuptial agreements and divorce settlements.

Marriage is the joining of two hearts, two lives, and two or more families together. Marriage is for better or for worse and in good times and bad times. At all costs, keep the anger out of your marriage, and make sure to forgive your partner often. This is easier said than done. Never go to bed angry.

Your previous single budgets will help with constructing your married budget. Hopefully, your future spouse believes in budgeting and has a working budget. (What are their spending habits and personal budgeting methods?) Use the same principles as in your single budget. Discuss future marital finances! There is no need to merge finances until after the wedding.

Before you say, "I do", there needs to be a conversation about finances, and a meeting of the minds. Find the answers to the following questions. Do you know your future spouse's financial goals, philosophy, and views on money? Do their spending habits include unlimited spending? Are they going to save every penny and never splurge? Is regularly loaning money to friends and family going to be their practice? Is borrowing money from mom, dad, grandmom, Derrick, Lisa, the bank,

152

credit card companies, and/or payday loans how some of their bills will be paid? What are your savings, credit score, and Fico scores? Is there a savings plan that allows them to be free to spend and enjoy the rest of their income? Does your future spouse constantly treat others to dinner and/or vacations? Is retirement planning in their budget plan? Have they ever filed for bankruptcy? The difficult questions must be asked! If the tough questions are not asked now, the knowledge of those delayed answers to those questions can be detrimental!

Before the discussion on money, there needs to be a discussion on gender roles. In the 1950s, the traditional gender roles included a stay-at-home mother who cooked all meals, completed most household chores, and raised the children, while the husband was the breadwinner or money maker. Today, some women still work inside the home, while others work outside, contributing to the breadwinning. Where is the balance on gender roles in your future household, and what do the gender roles look like? Do not assume anything. If preparing for marriage, get answers now!

Ask the right questions about money before heading to marriage. In pre-marital counseling sessions, finances must be discussed. Financial classes are often a great marriage builder too. In a class like this, a couple must work together as a team to manage their finances. The number one problem in a marriage is not infidelity (cheaters /adulterers), but major financial issues.

After having the conversation about money and finances, you and your future spouse are ready to make that sample budget. The married budget will also be a work in progress. Couples' finance meetings should be held at least one to two times a month. If need be, have weekly finance meetings. Each person is accountable to each other for how the household money is spent. Decide who will handle the numbers and finances. This assignment is not gender-driven. The one person who is great with finances, paying bills, budgeting, computer input into a spreadsheet or apps, should handle the finances, but not make all the decisions.

Pick a time and place for the financial couple's meeting and stick to it! Conversations about the household finances keep everyone informed and focused on the family's finances. Financial insecurity is like living on shaky ground. Having a healthy financial plan will enable a couple to eliminate many of the money issues that many couples experience. (This meeting is not a part of date night.)

During the financial conversation, discuss how the money was spent the previous month, talk about new goals, and revisit old ones, potential problems, and investments. Having a healthy financial plan and these types of discussions will help work out any problems within your budget, as well as allowing time for you and your partner to devise solutions to any financial problems. The finance meeting will help keep you on track, and hopefully help meet the family budget benchmarks. Keep a financial meeting log and have a money book or use an app to keep financial records. There are computer apps to assist with finances and budgeting practices.

Since there are many beliefs and philosophies on marital finances, establish one as a couple. One philosophy is "Your money, my money, and the household account". Another is, "I can do what I want with my money, and you do what you want with yours". How will the money be managed in this marriage? Yours, mine, or ours? Will there be separate bank accounts and a household account to pay bills? How will household bills be paid, and from what account? Will all the bills be joined together? Will the household bills be a 50/50 split or percentage based on each other's salary? Or will the husband pay all the bills and the wife's money is hers to do want she wants with it? Or will all the money go in one pot? Ask and answer these questions and create a financial philosophy before the wedding.

(For wedding planning advice and a sample wedding budget, see appendix 2.)

Money Tip
Couples may want to institute a money limit on purchases without the other's approval or consent.

(Some couples do not believe in this concept. But accountability around the family's finances is a key factor in financial stability.)

If you follow the above money tip, neither spouse will spend over a specific dollar limit without the other's consent. Each couple should determine the dollar limit that works best for the marriage. Therefore, this will help:

1. Eliminate unnecessary spending.
2. Give your partner a voice on major expenditures.
3. Help them adhere to the budget and goals.

Hopefully, with this in mind, your spouse will not come home from work with a brand new $40,000 car without any input from you. Choose the limit amount that works for your marriage, or decide that this is not important. Before the marriage, every couple should figure out what financial plan works best for them in their life ahead.

Some couples adhere to the principle, "Your money is your money, and my money is my money," and then they share household expenses. Once again, whatever works for each marriage, subscribe to it. This concept supports a spouse buying a new $40,000 car at their whim or discretion. There are many different viewpoints on money and marriage. Nonetheless, how money and bills will be managed must be discussed before saying "I do." The budget listed in this section is one budget for both spouses, with each having input from the other party. Financial viewpoints may change during the marriage. One way may not work for both people, and the handling of the finances will have to be modified.

If you fail to plan, you are planning to fail. Plan to succeed in your marriage!

The Beginning of Marriage

Congratulations! All of the wedding festivities are complete. Weddings can take months to years to plan, but some people forget to plan for life after the wedding and/or honeymoon.

Now begins the difficult task of joining two lives together in matrimony. Married life is not easy. Two people who may have been independent for some time are now joining their lives together with an official legally binding agreement or covenant of a marriage license. Two people from different families are joining their lives together in every aspect of the word. Successful marriages take work, and both parties must work at their marriage every day. As stated earlier, marriage is not 50-50. Each person must strive to give more than 100 percent and every day. Will this happen every day? I think not, but strive to go beyond. Often, one might experience a scale that is not equal. My belief is that it is the job of the husband is to provide and protect his wife and family.

Keep people out of your marriage. Other people and family members should not come in between you and your partner, making trouble with bad advice. Everyone has an opinion, but that does not mean you should take everyone's advice nor give them the space to give their opinion on your marriage.

Throughout your marriage, have date nights. In my marriage, there were many dates before we were married, and after we were, we continued to date each other.

Financial disharmony is the top issue in marriage. The second major problem that leads to divorce is infidelity. If you want to get married, please be faithful to your spouse. If you want multiple partners, stay single! Marriage is a committed relationship between two people—the same two people!

Marital Tips for a Long, Healthy Marriage

1. *Communication is key.*
2. *Honor, love, and respect each other.*
3. *Listen and choose to be selfless.*
4. *Respect monogamy and honor your marriage vows.*
5. *"Happy wife, happy life."*
6. *Have weekly or bi-monthly financial meetings.*
7. *Learn to compromise.*
8. *Strive for family harmony with the in-laws.*
9. *Stay out of debt and have great finances.*
10. *Keep others out of your marriage.*

Complete a married life budget and find out if two can live cheaper than one. It takes discipline to stick to a budget. There are many computer and online financial apps to assist couples with budgeting and finances.

Exercise #14: Married Life Budget

Month -	Estimated	Actual
Income (Net)		
Primary Job – wife		
Primary Job – husband		
Part-time Job		
Part-time Job		
Interest/Investments		
Other -		
Total Income		
Expenditures – Needs		
Savings/Emergency Fund		
Retirement Savings		
Tithe/ Charity		
Food		
Groceries		
Take Out – Restaurants		
Housing		
Rent/Mortgage		
HOA		
Rental-House Insurance		
Utilities		
Water		
Gas/Heat		
Electricity		
Transportation		
Car Note/ Public/ Rideshare		
Gasoline		
Car Maintenance		
Car Insurance		
Utilities		
Water		
Heat/Gas		
Electricity		

Month-	Estimated	Actual
Childcare/Education		
Health Insurance		
Other -		
Total Needs Expenditures		
Expenditures – Wants		
Clothes		
Dental Insurance		
Life Insurance		
Cell Phone		
Cable TV		
Internet - Wi-Fi		
Student Loans		
Personal Care/Toiletries		
Credit Card #1		
Yearly Gift Giving		
December Holiday /Christmas Gifts		
Pet Care		
Gym Membership		
Hairdresser/Barber		
Vacation		
Allowance		
Subscriptions/Streaming		
Entertainment		
Miscellaneous		
Other -		
Total Want Expenditures		
Total Needs and Wants Expenditures		
Total Money Left		

Exercise #15: Annual Gifts – Married Life

Budget Amount - $_____

We plan to buy gifts for the following people:

Name	Occasion	Gift	Cost	Date
Wife	Birthday			
Husband	Birthday			
	Our Anniversary			
Mom	Birthday			
Dad	Birthday			
Mom	Birthday			
Dad	Birthday			
Family-	Birthday			
Family-	Birthday			
Family-	Birthday			
Family-	Birthday			
Family-	Birthday			
Family-	Birthday			
	Parents' Anniversary			
Friend 1	Birthday			
Friend 2	Birthday			
	Wedding 1			
	Wedding 2			
Wife	Valentine's Day			
Husband	Valentine's Day			
	Graduation			
	Miscellaneous			
Total				

Exercise #16: Christmas/Holiday Gift List
Married Life

Budget Amount - $_____

We plan to buy Christmas/Holiday gifts for the following people:

Name	Gift	Cost	Date	Purchased
Wife				
Husband				
Mom				
Dad				
Mom				
Dad				
Grandparents				
Grandparents				
Family-				
Family-				
Family-				
Family-				
Friend 1				
Friend 2				
Total				

The above gift-giving budget lists must be modified to fit your family structure, circle of friends, lifestyle, and finances. There is no obligation to purchase gifts that you cannot afford.

Are you ready to move onto the next stage of life?

CHAPTER 8

Married with Children

I t is very important for newly married couples to build a solid foundation and spend time learning about each other for a few years before starting a family. These precious times alone with your spouse will not happen again until your children are grown and out of the house 18-25 years later. (No guarantees.)

Some couples start their new marital relationship with children that were conceived before marriage, from other relationships, adoption, or raising other people's children. Bringing children together from different relationships into a new marriage is called a blended family.

For many different reasons, some couples start a family right away because of preference, age, unplanned pregnancy, or health reasons. Others already have children before marriage. Children will change the atmosphere of marriage, as well as the family budget. Unfortunately, the government and/or your employer do not add additional money to your monthly salaries to help you take care of your children. However, there are federal tax credits for children under 18 and those in college until 26 years old.

Not every marriage will result in children. For many reasons, some couples will be childless, possibly because of the inability to afford children, low sperm counts, a couple's choice not to have children, or the wife's inability to conceive.

How many children do you want? Does your spouse even want children? Does your spouse have children from a previous relationship? Can you afford the costs of raising children? Why do you want children? What is your parenting style? What religion will the children be raised in? Will there be a stay-at-home parent? Are the children attending full-time daycare or part-time daycare? Will the children attend a public, religious, or private school for elementary, middle, and high school? Plan and begin to save for future college costs when the children arrive.

Questions, questions, and more questions will be asked. At the appropriate time during the dating stage, your partner and you should know the answers to each of these questions. Please do not ask these questions on the first date. Wait until you both get to know each and feel that the relationship is leaning towards marriage. The answers to the above questions must be known before marriage. It would be a shame to find out that your wife does not want children and that has always been a non-negotiable issue for your, or vice versa.

Most people want healthy, perfect children with high IQs. Unfortunately, this will not be everyone's experience. Children may need tutoring or remedial help in one or more educational subject matter. Tutoring may be an expense.

How much does it cost to raise a child? According to a Department of Agriculture study in 2015, it will cost a middle-class family $233,610, excluding college costs, to raise a child.[20] Children's expenditures must be accounted for in the Married with Children Budget. Every age group for children brings about different expenditures.

Infants/toddlers - diapers, Similac, daycare, babysitting, toys, clothes, baby food, immunizations, etc.

School-age - school tuition, clothes, school uniforms, food, Boy Scouts, Girl Scouts, dance tuition, sports fees, sports equipment, gymnastics, music lessons, school trips, before- and after-school care, etc.

Teenagers - school tuition, clothes, food, Boy Scouts, Girl Scouts, dance tuition, sports fees, sports equipment, allowance, prom, school dances, gymnastics, school class fees, standardized tests with application fees, college application fees, etc.

---

[20] Lion, Mark. "The Cost of Raising a Child", n.d., Accessed September 8, 2020. https://www.usda.gov/media/blog/2017/01/13/cost-raising-child

Please note, in your Married with Children or Single with Children Budgets that vacation expenses increase when children are present. Some hotel packages do not charge for children, but there are usually additional costs connected to the vacation. Research and plan!

Exercise #17: A Family Configuration

(Please name a make-believe family. Feel free to change the family configuration.)

For this exercise, the new family configuration includes, mom, dad, four-year-old son, and two-year-old daughter. (Both children entered this family during the marriage.) Choose the names of the family members.

The _____ Family
(Your Family Name)

Mom- _____ Dad- _____

Child 1 (son, 4 years old)

First Name - _____

Middle Name - _____

His name means - _____

Child 2 (daughter, 2 years old)

First name - _____

Middle Name - _____

Her name means - _____

Please choose your children's names with meanings! The Bible, books, websites have a wealth of knowledge about names, their origins, and their associated meanings.

Each child does not enter the world with a plan book or blueprint for child rearing and the handling of their individual personalities. Each child is unique with his/her DNA and genetics. However, there are some basic tenets to raising children. Children need structure with a prescribed schedule and a discipline plan created in love. Both parents should agree on child-rearing, discipline, and rules. If both parents do not subscribe to this, children figure out quickly which parent will give them what they want. Parents must work together as a team.

Every child is different and has different needs. Give your children what they need and sometimes what they want, but do not indulge them with all their wants. Children need structure with daily household chores, which should help instill a work ethic within them, along with a sense of community. Let your children help in the kitchen with age-appropriate tasks. Make sure extra-curricular activities do not overshadow family times, school work, and proper sleep. Time management is paramount while raising children.

At an early age, begin to teach your children about the value of money and give age-appropriate lessons on financial responsibility. Teach them to save, spend a little, and give charitably. Giving them the tools for handling money. During their lifetime, your children will watch you as you spend and invest money. Raise responsible financial children.

Stay on top of children's schoolwork, projects, educational progress, and get to know their teachers, friends, and classmates. As soon as you see a behavior problem and/or an academic weakness develop in your child at school, address it with your child and the teacher. Teach children about the responsibility and value of money and how to budget. Children should experience budgeting in the home. For example, as a family, we have budgeted $80.00 for dinner at our favorite restaurant. Choose your meals and beverages accordingly. How often can a family eat out each month? Your planned budget will dictate the answer.

Parents decide what is best for their child(ren). No parent is perfect, and when mistakes are made, learn from them. Always listen to your children. Children need their parents under divided attention. Look at them when they speak to you. Spend time with your children. Eating together as a family creates relationships, structure, and togetherness. Make memories with your children. Shared activities and experiences, vacations, traditions, cooking together help create great memories.

Electronics should not be at the dinner table, and this includes everyone. Family members should talk, fellowship, and eat together. Family time around the dinner table is a bonding time. There is research that states family meals have great benefits, socially, financially, and physically.[21]

Motherhood and fatherhood are an important journey in the lives of those who choose to experience them. Ask family members and friends who have children about how to raise them. There is much research about raising children and books written on the topic.[22] Take parenting classes, read, and research the art of parenting. Raising children is also a journey that is learned by experience. What works for one child may not work for another child.

Parenting Tips

1. Children want time spent with you and not with things.
2. Children learn by example. (Watch what you say and do.)
3. Be honest.
4. Never punish your child in anger.
5. Uplift and never demean your child.

---

[21] Penkalski, Julie. "The Importance of Family Mealtime", n.d., Accessed June 15, 2020. https://www.fcconline.org/the-importance-of-family-mealtime/.

[22] Dewar, Gwen. "Parenting Styles: An Evidence-based, Cross Culture Guide" n.d., Accessed June 15, 2020. https://www.parentingscience.com/parenting-styles.html.

Exercise #18: Family Name - _____

Snapshot of Family Finances

Salaries –
My Salary – (Choose 1)
College degree(s) - $40,000.00
High school diploma - $24,000.00
Part-time - $20,000.00
Stay at Home - $0.00 income

Spouse Salary – (Choose 1)
College degree(s) - $40,000.00
High school diploma - $24,000.00
Part-time - $20,000.00
Stay at Home - $0.00 income

Housing Purchase - (Choose 1)
New Construction House
Pre-existing home
Rent house or an apartment

Monthly payment - $_____
Children Daycare – (Choose 1)
$1,600 per month ($800 per child)
Stay at home with children

The New Home

Many people purchase homes at different times in their life stages. Since homeownership is a major responsibility, some people would rather rent an apartment, condo, or house for a while or forever. Some of the responsibilities of homeownership include taxes, maintenance, and upkeep. Some reasons people purchase homes are because of ownership, investment, freedom, legacy, no landlord, tax benefits, and it's what their parents did. For whatever your reason is, and if you can afford it, let's buy a home.

Homeowner Tip

Please note that as a responsible homeowner, you have a monthly commitment to the mortgage company, paying city/town taxes, paying HOA fees, and maintaining a house in good condition.[23]

Can I afford a home? Online mortgage calculators can give an amount on how much a person can afford to pay for a house. Other online calculators include rent vs. buy calculators, home affordability calculators, and mortgage calculators. The information results from these calculators will only give information based on what you put into the calculator. Just because a calculator or a bank has approved a certain dollar amount for a mortgage does not mean you have to purchase a home based on that amount. Do not select a mortgage higher than for what you have been approved. Choose a lesser amount for the mortgage. Calculators and banks often do not take into consideration one's charitable giving, budget constraints, tutoring, medical bills, etc. Do not cash strap your budget by trying to live above your means. Buying a home that is not

---

[23] "Be a Responsible Homeowner", n.d., Accessed April 18, 2020. https://www.knowyouroptions.com/buy-overview/be-a-responsible-homeowner.

affordable will create stress and a financial burden. Many variables can happen while paying a monthly mortgage that are not calculated in the approved mortgage amount. Ask the following questions before settling on a price point for the home. Can I afford to pay the monthly mortgage if:

1. my wife becomes pregnant and cannot work during the pregnancy because of health reasons?
2. overtime hours are no longer offered?
3. one of us loses a job, is laid off, a strike occurs, or a pandemic happens that shuts down the world?
4. one of us becomes disabled due to an accident or health issues?
5. extremely high or low temperatures double the heating or cooling bills?

Many professional people purchase homes in whatever life stage in which they find themselves. It is in your best interest to qualify for a home loan (mortgage) before beginning to look for a home. This pre-qualification will assist you in choosing the home you can afford.

Do not stretch your budget too far to get that dream home. "House poor" is a term that means that the monthly expenses for your home is an unduly large portion of your monthly salary, and consequently, you cannot afford to do other activities, such as vacations, eating out, attending entertainment events, buying designer clothes, and driving late-model cars, etc. Never purchase a home where the mortgage payment is more than 25% of your take-home monthly salary. What is wrong with a very affordable starter home? A dream home can come later. Make sure you have a clear, concise estimate of all the living costs in that new home.

Once again, home costs should be no more than 25% percent of your take-home (net) income. (Some believe in the high end of 30% of your take-home pay for housing costs.) Please do not figure on overtime or part-time jobs to assist with the mortgage. Do the calculations based on your primary, full-time job. If one of the two of you wants to be a stay-at-home parent in the future, re-evaluate and only use one income for the mortgage application. Some printed information or real estate agents may encourage the purchase of a home that is higher than 25% of your take-home income. Do not put pressure on your budget and finances with a mortgage that is difficult to sustain each month.

Only purchase a fixed, 15-year mortgage. A 30-year mortgage payment will have lower payments, but it will take twice as long to pay off the home. Also never consider balloon mortgages, variable rate mortgages, and adjustable-rate mortgages (ARM). These types of mortgages have interest rates that are not fixed over the life of the loan. Balloon mortgages may or may not have fixed interest rates, but no amortization. Research the problems with these mortgages, and stay away from them. Thank God my son showed his mortgage papers to his aunt and me before signing them. We were fortunate to catch my son's problematic adjustable-rate mortgage before he signed the papers on his first home. Some realtors and mortgage brokers will try to sell balloon mortgages, variable rate mortgages, and adjustable-rate mortgages (ARM) to clients. Variable rate mortgages' interest rates will change due to fluctuation of interest rates, and ARM mortgages will change and adjust due to the index. There are advantages and disadvantages to these loans, but the risk is too great. Closely read the documentation for each loan and beware!

Mortgage interest rates at the time of purchase affect the monthly mortgage payment. In 1980 during the recession, my fiancée and I purchased a home together at a 14% interest rate. We had good credit, but the economy was so bad. Interest rates have not been that high since the 1980s. At the time of printing, the housing interest rates are around 3.48APR for a 15-year fixed and 3.99 for a 30-year fixed. If you can pay cash for your home, you have conquered one of the greatest hurdles of one's life. Most people cannot afford to purchase a home with cash. Therefore, a mortgage or home loan is usually necessary. One can apply for a mortgage loan at a bank, credit union, and/or mortgage companies to purchase a home. On some occasions, the person who is selling the home can give the purchaser a loan or the parents of the purchaser can help or give the down payment for the house.

Affording a particular home has many variable costs. These variables include utilities, taxes, Home Owner Association (HOA) fees, Private Monthly Insurance (PMI), trash and waste pickup, and monthly mortgage cost. The monthly mortgage cost should be no more than 25 percent of your monthly take-home income. Putting a bigger down payment lowers the cost of the monthly mortgage. The PMI is usually between 0.5-1.0% of the mortgage. If the down payment is less than 20%, PMI costs will be included in the monthly mortgage. PMI protects the lender in case the purchaser defaults on the loan. A down payment of 20 percent of the purchase price eliminates the monthly PMI payment.

Your FICO score and credit report determine the interest rate of the home mortgage. Hopefully, both parties have great credit scores. Poor and fair credit scores will often increase the interest rate on the home mortgage and thus make the monthly payment rate higher than those with good and excellent scores. Much risk is involved for the mortgage company with those persons with low credit scores and/or bad credit. Therefore, the mortgage company will approve a mortgage with an interest rate based on the company's risks. If the risks are too high for the mortgage company, the probability of no approval is very high.

If one of the spouses has a low credit score, the couple may decide to only use the income and credit score of the higher score spouse for the qualification of a mortgage.

Purchase a house you can afford. (No more than 25% of your take-home pay.) Research everything about your possible future neighborhood. Check out the future neighborhood in the morning, noon, late at night, and on weekends. Get the facts on the real estate taxes, the crime rate, ratings of the schools in the neighborhood school district, and the utility costs per month before you purchase the house. Know the travel distance between your job and your house.

As soon as an offer is accepted, schedule a contingency house inspection before the final purchase of the home. Acquire a fixed mortgage loan for 15 years and not another kind. Know your credit score and rating before shopping for a house. Get preapproved for a home mortgage before shopping. Use a real estate lawyer for "closing" the sale of the house, because it's the lawyer's job to protect your interests at the closing of the transaction of your new home. I always used a real-estate lawyer, but some would rather not.

When my former spouse and I came home from our honeymoon, we were shocked to notice a leak in our roof. Sadly, we did not have a house inspection before purchase. Some of the wedding gift money went to putting on a new roof on our home. Heed my advice!

Sample items in a mortgage loan for a house purchase of $300,000 with a down payment of 10% ($30,000) with a 15-year fixed loan and interest rate of 3.19APR leaves a mortgage loan of $270,000.00 (Each state has different rules and regulations.)

Sample Monthly Mortgage Costs

Principal & Interest (3.19APR)	$	1,889.00
Property Taxes	$	378.00
Home Owners Insurance	$	233.00
Private Mortgage Insurance (PMI)	$	113.00
HOA fees	$	000.00

Possible Monthly Mortgage	$	2,613.00

Congratulations and welcome to your new home. Where do we go from here? Does the furniture from the old apartment have a place in the newly purchased house? Make the decision based on finances, not emotions. Purchase furniture with budgeted money from your favorite stores, but use Craigslist, eBay, or thrift stores to stretch your money. Ask family and friends if they have furniture they are not using, or wait until budgeted money is available to buy what you desire. Furniture does not count as an emergency, so do not use your emergency fund.

Being married with children comes with modifications to the budget. There are additional budget line items when children are in the picture. A sample budget is below.

Exercise #19: Married with Children Life Budget

Month -	Estimated	Actual
Income (Net)		
Primary Job – me		
Primary Job – spouse		
Part-time Job -		
Interest - Investments		
Other -		
Total Income		
Expenditures – Needs		
Savings/Emergency Fund		
Retirement Savings		
Tithe/Charity		
Food		
Groceries		
Take out – Restaurants		
Housing		
Rent/Mortgage		
HOA		
Rental/House Insurance		
Utilities		
Water		
Gas/Heat		
Electricity		
Transportation		
Car Note/Public/Rideshare		
Gasoline		
Car Maintenance		
Car Insurance		
Utilities		
Water		
Heat/Gas		

Month	Estimated	Actual
Electricity		
Childcare/Education		
Health Insurance		
Other -		
Total Needs Expenditures		
Expenditures – Wants		
Clothes		
Dental Insurance		
Life Insurance		
Cell Phone		
Cable TV		
Internet - Wi-Fi		
Student Loans		
Personal Care/Toiletries		
Credit Card #1		
Yearly Gift Giving		
Pet Care		
Gym Membership		
Hairdresser/Barber		
Vacation		
Allowance		
Subscriptions/Streaming		
Entertainment		
Miscellaneous		
Other -		
Total Want Expenditures		
Total Needs/Wants Expenditures		
Total Money Left		

Exercise #20: Annual Gifts - Married Life with Children

Budget Amount - $_____

We plan to buy gifts for:

Name	Occasion	Gift	Cost	Date	Purchased
Wife	Birthday				
Husband	Birthday				
	Our Anniversary				
Child 1	Birthday				
Child 2	Birthday				
Mom	Birthday				
Dad	Birthday				
Mom	Birthday				
Dad	Birthday				
Family-	Birthday				
Family-	Birthday				
Family-	Birthday				
Family-	Birthday				
Parents'	Anniversary				
Parents'	Anniversary				
Friend 1	Birthday				
Friend 2	Birthday				
	Wedding 1				
	Wedding 2				
	Valentine's Day				
	Valentine's Day				
	Graduation				
	Miscellaneous				
Total					

Exercise #21: December Holiday/Christmas Gift List
Married with Children

Budget Amount - $_____

We plan to buy Christmas/Holiday gifts for:

Name	Gift	Cost	Date	Purchased
Wife				
Husband				
Child 1				
Child 2				
Mom				
Dad				
Mom				
Dad				
Family-				
Family-				
Family-				
Friend 1				
Teacher 1				
Teacher 2				
Total				

The above gift-giving budget lists must be modified to fit your family structure, circle of friends, lifestyle, and finances. There is no obligation to purchase gifts that you cannot afford.

Are you ready to move onto the next stage of life?

CHAPTER 9

Possible Life Changes With the Three D's: Divorce, Disability, or Death

I n a perfect world, problems never happen. Unfortunately, in one's life, troubles can and will arise. We are not looking for troubles and problems, but they seem to find us.

Hopefully, this chapter will not be needed in your life experiences. However, you must plan for any contingency.

There are two ways to lose a spouse, and they both begin with a D. Divorce and death affect one's budget because a salary is taken out. Before divorce or death, prior plans should be in place. A personal saving plan in case of divorce should be in effect. Can you effectively live without your spouse's salary? Is there a life insurance policy on both spouses? Death can occur at any age. Be prepared in case of death. One of the hardest parts of grieving a death is not having enough money to meet your needs after the death of a spouse. Grieving and worrying where the money will come from to continue life is not a very happy place. Prepare in advance; get life insurance on each spouse. Upon the death of your spouse, you and/or your children may qualify for Social Security benefits.

Another word that begins with a D, and which will impact a personal budget, is a disability. If being partially or totally disabled keeps you from working a full-time job and/or a part-time job, your income is often reduced. There are two types of disability, short- and long-term disability. Purchase disability insurance while able, and later, if you qualify, Social Security Disability benefits will give you a monthly income. The Social Security office is equipped to help those who may need these benefits with the application process. Social Security disability lawyers represent and assist clients with the application process or fight the denial of those benefits.

The subject of divorce is not a pleasant or pleasurable one. Marriage is for a lifetime, but not all marriages survive. Divorce signifies the death of a marriage and a relationship. How to go through a divorce is not taught in high school or college, and parents usually do not teach their children the how-to's of divorce during their formative years. Hopefully, divorce will not be a part of your life. Just in case, please read the information below.

At all costs, try to keep your sanity during and after the divorce. Encourage yourself during this process by affirming yourself; get therapy, read helpful books, and journal daily. Place all financial records of both parties in a secure place. Copy all personal records and your children's too, i.e., birth certificates and Social Security cards, and put them in a safe place outside the home. (Please comply with all state rules on this matter.)

Although my marriage of twenty-one years resulted in divorce, I still believe in marriage and the tips for a happy marriage in Chapter 7. It takes two committed people to make a successful marriage. One spouse cannot fix a marriage by himself or herself. Sometimes I think what I would do if I could only rewrite the narrative of my story, but God has healed me of being in a failed marriage. In my book, *While in the Valley: Teachable Moments in a Difficult Place,* I include ten lessons that I learned while going through a separation and divorce.

While going through a divorce, looking for another relationship will not fix a failed marriage. Stay focused on getting out of the failed marriage. After the marriage has dissolved, heal from the past relationship. Healing takes time and everyone heals at a different rate. Seek counseling or personal therapy for you and your children. (I am sorry that I did not do this.) Read books. Join a support group for divorced people. As a facilitator at my church's separated and divorced support group, many people have been healed through our group support. Forgiveness allows one to move on with life without negative emotions. Forgive the other party even if they do not deserve it. Find new interests; I started playing tennis after my divorce.

During the divorce, remove your spouse's name as the beneficiary from all accounts, and change your will and living trust and remove their name unless you would like to bless your spouse upon your demise. Divorce is often a life-altering experience.

Dating Again

Returning to single life after the marriage has legally dissolved may include dating again. Dating again should only begin when you are healed from the failed marriage and divorce. Do not try to fix a marriage with a new partner nor get a new partner to get over your old spouse. Please wait for the divorce to be legally finalized and until you are healed from the hurts of the marriage and divorce before dating again. Since healing takes time, allow yourself the time to heal.

The world of dating may have changed a little or a lot since you were first married. Dating, here we go again! Revisit the dating principles in Chapter 6. If the marriage was not successful, before trying again, be introspective and find out why the married failed.

Your Finances

During a divorce, death, or disability, your finances will possibly drastically change. The loss of your spouse's income will affect the budget. Spousal support and/or child support may be awarded to you, or you may be the one to pay it out. The non-custodial parent usually pays child support, and the greater the income, usually the greater the amount. Every situation and state laws differ.

It is your responsibility to provide for your family during a divorce, death, or disability. Disability insurance assists with meeting monthly bills if you are unable to work. Adequate life insurance is a safety net that provides for the family in case of death. In case of death, the money from the life insurance policy will aid a family with the loss of an income. A wise adult purchases life and homeowner's insurances to protect his or her family. Life does not always go as planned. One car accident can result in death or disability and will change lives in a matter of seconds. Plan accordingly.

Once again, the budget must be modified when divorce, death, or disability have occurred. For one, an income from the former spouse may be lost or reduced. Spousal support, child support, Social Security disability, or money from an insurance policy is not immediate. There is no divorce insurance in case of a split from a spouse. The loss of an income can derail one's budget and financial stability. Once again, an emergency fund is very important to have in place in case of emergencies. No one knows the exact time or probability of death, disability, or divorce. Be prepared just in case! Plan accordingly.

Exercise #22: Divorced/Widowed/Disabled Life Budget

Month -	Estimated	Actual
Income (Net)		
Primary Job		
Part-time Job		
Interest – Investments		
Spousal & Child Support		
Social Security/Disability		
Total Income		
Expenditures – Needs		
Savings/Emergency Fund		
Retirement Savings		
Tithe/Charity		
Food		
Groceries		
Take out – Restaurants		
Housing		
Rent/Mortgage		
HOA		
Rental/House Insurance		
Utilities		
Water		
Gas/Heat		
Electricity		
Transportation		
Car Note/Public/Rideshare		
Gasoline		
Car Maintenance		
Car Insurance		
Utilities		
Water		
Heat/Gas		

Month-	Estimated	Actual
Electricity		
Childcare/Education		
Other-		
Total Needs Expenditures		
Expenditures – Wants		
Clothes		
Dental Insurance		
Life Insurance		
Cell Phone		
Cable TV		
Internet - Wi-Fi		
Student Loans		
Personal Care/Toiletries		
Credit Card #1		
Yearly Gift Giving		
December Holiday/Christmas Gifts		
Pet Care		
Gym Membership		
Hairdresser/Barber		
Vacation		
Allowance		
Subscriptions/Streaming		
Entertainment		
Miscellaneous		
Other -		
Total Want Expenditures		
Total Needs/Wants Expenditures		
Total Money Left		

Exercise #23: Annual Gifts
Divorced/Widowed/Disabled

Budget Amount - $_____

I/we plan to buy gifts for:

Name	Occasion	Gift	Cost	Date	Purchased
Wife	Birthday				
Husband	Birthday				
	Our Anniversary				
Child 1	Birthday				
Child 2	Birthday				
Mom	Birthday				
Dad	Birthday				
Mom	Birthday				
Dad	Birthday				
Family-	Birthday				
Family-	Birthday				
Family-	Birthday				
Parents	Anniversary				
Parents	Anniversary				
Friend 1	Birthday				
Friend 2	Birthday				
	Wedding 1				
	Wedding 2				
	Valentine's Day				
	Valentine's Day				
	Graduation				
	Miscellaneous				
Total					

Exercise #24: December Holiday/Christmas Gift List
(Divorced/Widowed/Disabled)

Budget Amount - $_____

I/we plan to buy Christmas/ Holiday gifts for the following people:

Name	Gift	Cost	Date	Purchased
Wife				
Husband				
Family-				
Family-				
Family-				
Family-				
Family-				
Family-				
Family-				
Family-				
Friend				
Friend				
Total				

The above gift-giving budget lists must be modified to fit your family structure, circle of friends, lifestyle, and finances. There is no obligation to purchase gifts that you cannot afford.

Are you ready to move onto the next stage of life?

CHAPTER 10

Retirement Living

You must plan for every stage in your life. Congratulations! Retirement is now your life! Retirement is when a person stops working a full-time job because they have reached the governmental age to do so and/or have the necessary monetary funds to live without working. Retirement can begin at any age, but everyone does not make it to retirement because of death or the inability to afford it. Some people are forced to retire because of poor health. Retirement is not a waiting period for death. Now is the time to explore your interests, travel, start a new career, or volunteer.

As soon as you acquire your first job as a young person, you must begin to think and plan for retirement. Retirement can last for various amounts of years. Unfortunately, for some, retirement lasts only six months because of death or not enough retirement funds to live on. For others, retirement could be as long as thirty-five years or longer.

One should only retire when one has enough money to support their lifestyle for the rest of their life and is emotionally ready to leave an occupation. Retirement is not an age. Retirement can happen in your 20s, 30s, 40s, 50s, 60s, or 70s. Your retirement age is predicated upon your financial situation. Based on the Age Discrimination in Employment Act in the U.S., there is no mandatory age for retirement. In spite of this law, forced retirement sometimes occurs. Forced retirement occurs when someone's company closes or downsizes and the employee is unable to get another job at the company. The senior citizen is forced to retire earlier than planned. At this juncture in their lives, many senior citizens are forced to apply for their Social Security benefits and begin using their retirement funds.

Early retirement is retiring before the age of 65. Health benefits from another source are needed because Medicare, which involves some healthcare benefits, does not begin until age 67, although financial benefits can begin at 62 years of age from Social Security.

What happens during retirement? Firstly, during retirement, the retiree does not have to wake up each morning and go to a place of full-time employment. This is a blessing. Secondly, the retiree determines each day what happens to their time and day. Be careful not to allow others to fill up your days with their expectations. Be active during retirement. Retirement does not mean staying at home every day and doing nothing. Volunteer, learn new hobbies, revisit old interests, give more time to current hobbies, visit family and friends, learn a new musical instrument, explore new interests, and travel. Consider having one day a week called "My Day". On this day, it's all about you. No errands or favors for anyone. Relax and do what you want to do.

Many retirees choose to babysit their grandchildren or offer transportation to and from daycare or school. Others offer after-school care for their grandchildren or other people's children. There are senior groups that offer travel, daily activities, and social events. In retirement, every day is Saturday, and what does not get done today can be completed tomorrow.

Medicare is a governmental healthcare benefit beginning at 65 years of age. The application for Medicare benefits must be in place before your 65th birthday or submit to a financial penalty.

Medicare Part A is administered by the US government and pays 80 percent of all medical bills, and Medicare Part B, the other 20 percent, is the responsibility of the Medicare patient. Supplemental D health insurance will pay the remaining 20 percent if the senior citizen purchases the policy. Not purchasing supplemental D health insurance can be financially detrimental if a major illness occurs in one's life.

Social Security is a benefit for senior citizens who have paid into a Social Security account while working a job(s). Most employers send a portion of an employee's salary to the Social Security government agency. The government then puts the monies into a fund until the age requirement is met and ready for disbursements. Age requirements for full and partial disbursements vary according to a person's birthdate. The US government desired to have Social Security benefits to be a supplemental stream of income in retirement. The US government did not plan for its citizens to live on their Social Security benefit alone. Social Security income is **not** enough to live on each month, and it is a taxed benefit. Refer to www.ssa.gov website for additional information and qualifications on benefits. Also, consult your tax preparer, accountant, and/or financial planner. Other Social Security benefits include disability, survivorship, and supplemental.

The problem with this is that the United States Social Security system is a broken-down system, and there may not be enough in the Social Security fund to give benefits to millennials and those after them. Plan now for additional streams of income just in case the funds are not present when needed.

During retirement, some retirees begin a second career, start new businesses, and/or turn their hobbies into a business. Having a steady income via a pension, Social Security, and/or annuities allows a retiree to explore new options, careers, and businesses. Some retirees return to work full- or part-time after retiring because of boredom and needing activities to fill their days. The saddest part of retirement is those retirees having to return to work because their expenses outweigh their retirement income and they need to make additional money.

What will be your living arrangements during retirement? There are many options. Some choose to stay in their house; others choose to downsize and purchase a smaller home or condo. Renting an apartment is a choice for many. Renting as a senior citizen means there are no responsibilities of fixing broken items in the home and shoveling snow. Assisted living facilities and senior housing are other viable options. Assisted living is not a nursing home. However, this type of living helps the senior with cooked meals, daily activities, and with basic personal care. Finally, some retirees move in with their children, for many different reasons. One reason is to help their children raise their children, and another is for financial reasons for either party.

How much is needed to live a comfortable life during retirement? Each retiree has different financial needs. Online retirement income calculators are available to assist with determining the amount of money that is needed until the end of one's life. People are living longer and living well into their 80s and 90s, and even living past 100 more and more frequently.

One must have enough money to make it to the end of life. No one wants to go back to work at 95 years old.

There is no set time for retirement. It can be as long as you want it to be or as short as you want it to be. It is a choice. While in your twenties, please plan for retirement. If a person chooses to wait until their 50s to start saving for retirement, they would have to save a very large sum of money from their income in order to account for the shortness of time.

How will you live during retirement? What monetary funds will be available to support your daily lifestyle? Once again, one should start planning for retirement as soon as you receive your first job in your twenties. Some of my friends have been retired longer than they have worked at their full-time job. There are several monetary vehicles one can use as additional streams of income to aid them in their retirement. Invest in your future.

A 401K is a retirement investment vehicle that is sponsored by the employer with pre-taxed money from the employee's paycheck. The beauty of this plan is that some employers match dollar for dollar that employees put in from their salary up to a certain amount. Take advantage of this wonderful employee benefit.

A 403B is another retirement investment vehicle, but it is a fund for nonprofit organizations' employees. Money from a 401K and 403B are from your untaxed money deposited directly from your paycheck from your employer into your investment account. The money gains interest while in the account. Money earned from these accounts cannot be taken out until age 59½ without a major penalty. Save for the long haul.

A Roth IRA is an after-tax investment plan for retirement. The interest made from the growth of stocks, bonds, and mutual funds is another source of income in retirement.

During my first teaching job at the age of twenty-two, one of the approved school district financial companies' representatives asked if I wanted to have a conversation about retirement financial planning. What? I am twenty-two years old and single with no children. Unfortunately, I did not have that conversation until many years later. Big mistake! A future begins with a person's very first major employment. If possible, start saving immediately through the employer for retirement. I had that option at 22-years old, but I did not take the opportunity. What did I do with that money? I do not know.

There are many decisions to make when stepping up to this next stage of life. However, many of these decisions have to be made years in advance of retirement. Will you remain in your present home or purchase a home in a retirement community? Or will you downsize and sell your big home and move to an apartment, condominium (condo), or a smaller home? Will you remain in your present state, move to another state with a warmer climate, or move to a state with a lower cost of living? Or will you sell everything and move in with your children?

Having a mortgage on a fixed income during retirement can be a burden. Soon after I retired, the mortgage was paid. This freed up a great portion of my budget. I did not have a mortgage-burning event because I did not want everyone to know I had extra money. Do you want 20-25 percent of your retirement income leaving via a mortgage payment? Nonetheless, some retirees choose to rent after selling their home or just rent instead of owning a home. What is the best situation? Retirees must do what is right for their circumstances. Be mindful that your retirement funds must be able to support your living arrangement. At every stage of life, you must make decisions. In this retirement stage of life, you may be single, widowed, divorced, or married.

Everyone does not make it to retirement, due to deciding to continue to work, health, death, or poor finances. However, we must prepare for retirement as soon as possible, because we do not know what life will bring to each of us. What will I do when I retire? Plan now!

Before signing the papers for retirement, do the research three to five years in advance. Ask co-workers, HR department, family, friends, and workshops about the steps for retiring in your company. Before leaving the job, make sure there is enough money to live on, especially for those possible three months from the date of retirement and the arrival of the first check from the pension board, annuity, and/or Social Security office.

Make sure all paperwork is in order and received by the necessary offices by the correct due date. In my case, my school district had my signed official paperwork for retirement, but the state education pension board never received their official paperwork. Call, inquire, and send emails to the necessary offices about the paperwork and documents that are needed for retirement. If there is a problem with the above, loss of wages, change of retirement dates, and other unfortunate things can happen. Double and triple check all information and advice received from people. There is a great deal of information to process before that last day of work and your new retired life.

Enjoy your retirement. Live the life you want to live. Set boundaries for your time with family, friends, and others. Spend your money wisely, because it has to last until your death or the end of the world. Continue to live on a budget. Travel any time you want, especially in the off-travel season. Learn a musical instrument or continue lessons on a previous instrument.

Now is the time to join senior groups, senior travel groups, and senior centers. These groups have many activities and trips. Please volunteer your time to non-profit organizations and/or to your place of worship. In retirement, some type of activity outside of the home must occur. This stage of life is not the time to wait for death; it is the time to live life on your terms and not on those of your employers or others! Remember, for various reasons, not everyone will make it to retirement. Retirement is a blessing; enjoy it.

Exercise #25: Budget - Retirement Living

Month -	Estimated	Actual
Income (Net)		
Pension –		
Social Security		
Part-time Job		
Annuities		
Spouse Income/Pension		
Interest - Investments		
Social Security		
Total Income		
Expenditures - Needs		
Savings/Emergency Fund		
Retirement Savings		
Tithe/Charity		
Food		
Groceries		
Take Out - Restaurants		
Housing		
Rent/Mortgage		
HOA		
Rental/House Insurance		
Utilities		
Water		
Gas/Heat		
Electricity		
Transportation		
Car Note/ Public/Rideshare		
Gasoline		
Car Maintenance		
Car Insurance		
Health Insurance		

Month -	Estimated	Actual
Other-		
Total Need Expenditures		
Expenditures – Wants		
Clothes		
Dental Insurance		
Life Insurance		
Cell Phone		
Cable TV		
Internet - Wi-Fi		
Student Loans		
Personal Care/Toiletries		
Credit Card #1		
Yearly Gift Giving		
Christmas Gifts		
Pet Care		
Gym membership		
Hairdresser/Barber		
Vacation		
Allowance		
Subscriptions/Streaming		
Entertainment		
Miscellaneous		
Other -		
Total Want Expenditures		
Total Needs & Wants		
Total Money Left		

Exercise #26: Annual Gifts – Retirement Living

Budget Amount - $_____

I/we plan to buy gifts for:

Name	Occasion	Gift	Cost	Date
Wife	Birthday			
Husband	Birthday			
Wife	Valentine's Day			
Husband	Valentine's Day			
	Our Anniversary			
Mom	Birthday			
Dad	Birthday			
Child 1	Birthday			
Child 2	Birthday			
Grandchild	Birthday			
Grandchild	Birthday			
Family-	Birthday			
Family-	Birthday			
Family-	Birthday			
Friend 1	Birthday			
	Wedding 1			
	Wedding 2			
Wife	Valentine's Day			
Husband	Valentine's Day			
	Graduation			
	Miscellaneous			
Total				

Exercise #27: December Holiday/Christmas Gift List
Retirement Living

Budget Amount - $_____

I/we plan to buy Christmas/ Holiday gifts for the following people:

Name	Gift	Cost	Date	Purchased
Wife				
Husband				
Mom				
Dad				
Mom				
Dad				
Grandchild				
Grandchild				
Grandchild				
Family-				
Family-				
Family-				
Family-				
Family-				
Family-				
Family-				
Family-				
Total				

The above gift-giving budget lists must be modified to fit your family structure, circle of friends, lifestyle, and finances. Gifts for your spouse can be purchased from allowance funds also. There is no obligation to purchase gifts that you cannot afford.

Part IV

How Will I Do Life?

CHAPTER 11

"What if?"
You make the decision!

W hat if this happens? What if that happens? What should I do? With your new-found knowledge, ask yourself if you are making a financially responsible decision. Read the scenarios below and make a good financial decision.

Scenario 1

It's December 5th, and your washing machine has stopped working. A repairman has assessed the problem with the washing machine, and he recommends that it is not cost-effective to fix it. What decision should you make?

1. Ask your parents for $500.00 to purchase a new one.
2. Use your emergency fund to purchase a new one.
3. Go to the nearest department store and place the new washing machine on your credit card.

4. Buy a used washing machine from Craigslist, eBay, or thrift store with your emergency savings.

5. Use the neighborhood laundromat until a new washing machine is affordable.

Scenario 2

Your friends want to go on vacation to Barbados next summer. It will cost $799, plus spending money. Is this trip affordable at this time?

1. Put the cost of the trip on MasterCard or Visa and pay the credit card company every month until paid.
2. Use your $800 budgeted vacation money from your budget.
3. Borrow from friends and family.
4. Do not go on the trip because you cannot afford it.
5. Save for the trip and take it next year.
6. Go to the nearest beach for a day trip instead.

Scenario 3

Your 10-year-old car needs a transmission. What decision should you make about the car?

1. Get a rebuilt transmission for $2,000.00.
2. Buy a new car and incur a monthly car note.
3. Buy a used car from your savings.
4. Take public transportation until you can afford any of the above.
5. Carpool to work with co-workers and/or use car-share companies (i.e., Uber, Lyft).

Scenario 4

Your son's eighth-grade class is going on a day ski trip. The trip is $100. Payment is due immediately. Only 75 spots are available. The first 75 students with full payment will receive a spot on the trip. What choice(s) is the right decision?

1. Immediately send the money to school for the trip from your budgeted savings.
2. You pay half of the cost and your son pays half of the cost.
3. Your son pays the total cost of the trip from his savings.
4. Your son is unable to go because the budget has not allowed for this particular trip.
5. Borrow the money for the trip from another fund in the budget plan.

Scenario 5

The living room needs a new sofa, and a popular department store is having a holiday sale. This sofa will be perfect in the living room. What decision should you make about the sofa?

1. Go to the department store and purchase the sofa.
2. Yes, the sofa is waiting for you at the store. Use your budgeted funds and purchase the sofa.
3. Wait until you save enough money to purchase the sofa, and buy it at that time.
4. Purchase the sofa on a "three easy payments" plan with zero-interest for three months.
5. After careful thought, a new sofa is not needed at this time.

The answers, tips, and reasoning to the above scenarios are found below.

The Correct Answers and Reasoning

Tip
If the money is budgeted for the following items, use it. How much of your savings do you want to use?

Scenario 1   Broken Dryer

1. **Do not** ask your mom or dad for $500.00 to purchase a new one because you are standing on your own, independently.
2. Yes, use the emergency fund money to purchase a brand-new washing machine.
3. Do **not** go to the nearest department store and put the new washing machine on a credit card because the funds are not available. Use cash only.
4. If some of the cash funds are available, buy a used washing machine from Craigslist, eBay, or a thrift store.
5. Choices #2 and #4 are valid.

Scenario 2   Barbados Vacation

1. **Do not** put the cost of the trip on MasterCard or Visa if you cannot pay it off when it is due.
2. Yes, use the vacation money from your vacation budget.
3. Do **not** borrow from friends and family, because you are an independent person. Do not depend on other people's money to fund your needs and wants.
4. Vacations are **not** only for the rich, but also for those who can afford them.
5. Save for the trip and take it next year.
6. Go to the nearest beach for a day trip instead.

Scenario 3   Car Down!

1. According to how much the car is worth, possibly get a rebuilt transmission for $2,000.00.
2. If the cash funds are available, buy it. If you must, finance a car with low monthly car payments for three years or less.
3. Yes, buy a used car from your savings.
4. Yes, take public transportation until an affordable car can be purchased.
5. If possible, carpool to work with co-workers and/or if you can afford it, use car-share companies (i.e., Uber, Lyft).

Scenario 4   Eighth Grade Ski Trip

1. Yes, send the money to school for the trip from your budgeted savings.
2. You can also pay half of the cost and your child can pay half of the cost from your budgets.
3. Yes, your child can pay the total cost of the trip from their savings.
4. If the funds are not available and there is no room in the budget, your child will be **unable** to go on the ski trip.
5. You cannot borrow from another fund in the budget.

Scenario 5   New Living Room Sofa

1. The budget does not allow for the new sofa.
2. Yes, use the budgeted funds and purchase the sofa.
3. Wait until you save enough to purchase the sofa.
4. Beware and be careful! The "three easy payments" plan with no interest is super risky. If a payment is missed or late, the interest jumps from 0 to a high percent
5. There is nothing wrong with deciding you do not need a new sofa at this time.

CHAPTER 12

A Letter to My Younger Self

D ear Marlene,

I pray this letter finds you in great health and abundant joy. Over these last 40 years, I have learned a great deal about life, money, marriage, rearing children, debt, life balance, friends, and family. I am so grateful for raising two beautiful, smart, ambitious children, thankful for the family, friends, and people in my life, the 34-year-long rewarding teaching career, my music ministry and songs I have composed, and the three books I've written.

First, I am so glad that you went to college, finished debt-free in four years, and received your teaching dream job right after your May college graduation for that upcoming fall school year. As a single teacher, you were overjoyed that you completed your master's in music education before getting married. Although you wanted a master's in conducting, you were still blessed with your second choice. Traveling all over the world as a single young woman with friends and family broadened your horizons and introduced you to many different cultures.

However, as I look back over my life, I wish some things would have been done differently. Although you accomplished almost every goal that you had in mind at the time, I wished you had additional pre-marital counseling sessions before marrying who you thought was the love of your life. Do not ignore red flags before marriage that do not match your values, spiritual beliefs, or views on money. Never borrow money from your 401K for anything, buy expensive cars, and take out personal loans, but purchase everything with cash or pay off the bill when it arrives. Spend less than you make and save the rest! You learned this important lesson after your divorce. As a child, your parents gave you a great financial understanding of savings and spending, but not on investments. They had no knowledge of investments and saving for retirement in a 401K or 403B. Although you did not save the money in your twenties and thirties as you should have, I thank God, with education, you figured money management and retirement savings out before it was too late.

As a retiree, I am blessed to live the lifestyle I want to live because you managed to put your financial house in order. I live in a debt-free house, a paid-for car, and have no balances on credit cards or loans. Living with all that prior debt was a heavy,

heavy burden. Money from every paycheck was going to pay your debtors, and this was not a wealth-building strategy. In your forties, with financial education, you figured it out. Because you had a part-time job(s) your entire adult life, the part-time job(s) afforded you the ability to pay for your children's undergraduate college educations at Harvard and Hampton University, pay additional bills, make repairs on the house, purchase cars, and take yearly vacations. At this juncture in life, I am glad you did what you wanted to do in life and blessed that you made the best decisions you could at the time. Saving additional money for retirement was the one goal you did not complete.

And now, because of what I have learned in life, I can remind others to love God, family, and be true to themselves. Live without debt, spend less, do not try to impress others, and live! Plan, budget, and be disciplined. Keep your body healthy. Eat right, exercise daily, and get enough sleep each night. Keep God in your life. Blessings.

Sincerely,

Marlene Jenkins Cooper

Exercise #28: Write a Letter to Your Future Self

Write to your future self about your accomplishments, fulfilled dreams, completed aspirations, and who you hope to be in 20, 30, or 40 years from today.

CHAPTER 13

Epilogue
It's Your Life, Decisions, and Choices

L ife is about choices; the choices you make result in the good or bad consequences that follow. Specific life decisions and choices will determine your future. Challenges, challenges, and more challenges may and will occur. How will you handle them?

Unfortunately, you will probably make some bad choices during your life journey. However, failure does not mean that your life is over. Mistakes and missteps will happen. Get up, dust yourself off, start anew, and recover. Face your failures and learn from them. Remember to research, plan, budget, and save. The rewards of living a stress-free life are endless. For one, a good, restful night's sleep is priceless. Who wants to worry all night about how the bills will be paid and where the money will come from?

Life 101: Money Management and Adulting Made Simple, contains tools to help young adults make informed decisions and good choices. Adulting is not easy, but it is doable. Others have gone before you and are living the adulting life. At twenty-three, I wished I would have done everything that I've written about in this book. Hindsight is 20/20. If I had only known about all the above information while in my twenties, I would have made different choices.

Final Words

For multiple reasons, those who are single, single with children, married, married with children, disabled, or divorced sometimes feel the need to return to their parents' house for lodging. If this happens, breathe, gather your thoughts, and plan to leave as soon as possible to live on your own.

Since you are reading this book, please learn from my mistakes, my knowledge, and my revelations on life. It's easy to do nothing and let life happen. As a wife and parent, I did not always make the best choices and decisions. I made mistakes, and you will too. I believe I have learned from my mistakes and work diligently to fix them. Ask questions of the elders in your family and community, research the answers to your questions, and then decide using the answers you receive.

Remember to respect the law, respect your elders, and be a good friend to your friends. Please do not eat all of your money in restaurants, wear all your money on your back, and drive in a car that constantly takes all your money. Plan, budget, and be disciplined.

In spite of good financial habits and choices, your road will still possibly have many twists and turns, blunders, and challenges. Having a plan keeps one ahead of money pitfalls and challenges. It is important to subscribe to a personal budget and stick to it. Subscribing to a plan takes self-discipline. I still struggle with my single person food budget. I can afford to spend $600.00 a month on food from the supermarket, but why?

I am overjoyed to be free of debt. The weight of debt is a physical as well as a mental burden. Recently, I lost 82.5 pounds, and it was a heavy physical burden on my body. Now, with the loss of fat, my steps are much lighter, and I feel and look great! I have learned that, "Nothing tastes as good as thin feels".

Statistics are very high on the return of weight and debt. Sticking to the lifestyle changes, food plans, and personal budget will keep your debt and weight down. Yes, I may make modifications to my food plan at times, but I have a food plan. My next big goal is to have my home clutter-free.

Take life as it comes. Do not be afraid or nervous. There will be instances when unforeseen events and life's circumstances will challenge your budget plan. This is why an emergency fund is needed and important. Plan for emergencies,

221

because unplanned events will happen. An emergency can cost as low as $40 for a refrigerator condenser fan motor part to $15,000 for a brand-new roof. No plan is full proof, but have a plan in place for emergencies. Take the necessary steps to ensure financial security for you and your family. Also keep emergency cash in a secret, accessible location. In the summer of 2003, my 19-year-old daughter was living in New York City during a blackout with no electricity and no use of Automatic Teller Machines (ATM). Therefore, my daughter had no access to her money. I was on a cruise and only could watch the events on the cruise TV. Cash was king! Thank God; she survived it.

Eight months before the publication of *Life 101: Money Management and Adulting Made Simple,* the COVID 19 pandemic occurred throughout the entire world. Only essential businesses remain open for business, and everyone had to remain in their homes except for essential workers. Schools and all other businesses were to shut down worldwide. Jobs were lost, businesses failed, and the world struggled to keep people alive. During this time, an emergency fund and a healthy body with no diseases were of the utmost importance. Some countries gave their citizens money to live on, and the United States government bailed out many businesses and helped Americans with a stimulus check of $1,200 who made less than $75,000 per year. Unfortunately, this worldwide pandemic is not over as of November 1, 2020.

"If at first, you don't succeed, try, try, again." This proverb is attributed to Thomas H. Palmer and Frederik Maryat. If you fail, get up and try again. You can succeed at anything you want to do. But remember this quote by John J. Berkley: "Most people don't plan to fail; they fail to plan."

Hopefully, *Life 101* has prepared you and given you a wealth of knowledge about money management, life, and adulting. There are no excuses. The world makes money off of the ignorance of people. Read, research, and plan. Tax codes and financial policies change. Ask a financial professional about tax questions and investments.

Be mindful of changeable financial trends. However, have a planned budget with options to modify. Have a financial plan and stick to it. The road to a financially healthy life and your pathway to freedom is true discipline. Money matters! Respect it and make informed decisions about life and your money. Live life without debt and strive to be financially independent.

The game of life and the adulting process will never end until the very end. Make the right choices. Control yourself in every area of your life. It is not how you start, but how you finish. Finish well. Good luck with life, the tools to win with money, and the strategies to be a successful adult. May your life be full of many blessings, and may you make great decisions on money and life. Win at life and happy adulting!

Appendix 1

Etiquette

Practicing Good Manners

A. Arrive on-time to events.

B. RSVP means please respond if you are coming or if you are unable. This is from a French term, *Répondez s'il vous plaît*. Please commit to your reply.

C. Use good manners.

D. Shake with a firm handshake.

E. Greet others with a good morning.

F. Let your word be your bond. (Do what you said you will do.)

G. Send thank you notes for gifts received. (Older people like handwritten thank you notes.)

Appendix II

Planning a Wedding

A wedding is a wonderful celebration, and the average wedding costs about $30,000. Your wedding does not have cost $30,000 or more. Create a budget for your wedding and stick to it. Use cash for everything. Only use the money that you have saved, budgeted, and/or gifted. Please do not put your wedding on credit cards or apply for a personal loan to pay for it. What is the cost of your dream wedding? Can you afford it, or what will you have to modify to be able to afford it?

Wedding Budget

Date	Typical Cost	Estimated	Actual
Wedding Dress	$2000-10000		
Ceremony (Church)	$700-$1500		
Wedding Dress	$5000-$7000		
Officiant (minister)	$200-$350		
Organist	$200-$250		
Flowers	$2500-$3000		
Wedding Favors	$350-$500		
Event Space	$5000-$7000		
Catering	$100-$125 pp		
Wedding Cake	$500- $1000		
Limousine	$800-$1000		
Orchestra/Band/DJ	$3500-$4500		
Photographer	$2500-$5000		
Invitations	$350-$500		
Videographer	$1200-$2000		
Total Cost			

Appendix III

Household Chores

Bedroom	Chores
Daily	Make bed
	Place clothes in the closet/ dresser drawers
	Place dirty clothes in the hamper
Weekly	Sweep/vacuum floor
	Change bed sheets weekly
Kitchen	
Daily	Wash dishes, pots, and pans
	Wipe countertop and kitchen table
	Sweep floor
Weekly	Clean out refrigerator
	Mop kitchen floor
	Empty trash can (or as needed)
Bathroom	
Daily	Clean sinks and countertop
	Clean tub and shower
	Soiled towels & washcloths in the hamper
Weekly	Empty trash can
	Sweep and mop floor
	Wipe mirror
	Clean toilet
Laundry	
Weekly	White Clothes
	Dark Clothes
	Light Colored Clothes

Appendix IV

Weekly Menu Planner

	Sun.	Mon.	Tues.	Wed.
Breakfast				
Protein				
Grain				
Vegetables				
Fruit				
Beverage				
Healthy oil				
Lunch				
Protein				
Grain				
Carbohydrate				
Vegetables				
Fruit				
Beverage				
Healthy oil				
Dinner				
Protein				
Grain				
Carbohydrate				
Vegetables				
Beverage				
Healthy oil				

Remember portion control and serving amounts, and note the weight of each food item on the plate.

Weekly Menu Planner

	Thu.	Fri.	Sat.
Breakfast			
Protein			
Grain			
Vegetables			
Fruit			
Beverage			
Healthy oil			
Lunch			
Protein			
Grain			
Carbohydrate			
Vegetables			
Fruit			
Beverage			
Healthy oil			
Dinner			
Protein			
Grain			
Carbohydrate			
Vegetables			
Beverage			
Healthy oil			

Remember portion control, serving amounts, and note the weight of each food item on the plate.

EXERCISES

INDEX

Marlene Jenkins Cooper is an author, publisher, musician, and retired public school teacher. *Life 101: Money Management and Adulting Made Simple* is her third book. Her other books include *While in the Valley: Teachable Moments in a Difficult Place* and *Grace Notes: Five-Minute Inspirational Devotionals for the Church Choir, Musician, and Friends of Music.* During her thirty-four years of teaching service, she not only held the general vocal music teacher position but later also became a computer specialist.

As a 13-week course, the author used her *Life 101* curriculum to teach her students about money management, life stages, and how to make wise decisions in the future. Today, many of her former students are using what they learned from this class as adults.

Ms. Cooper holds degrees from Temple University and The King's College. She is the parent of two adult children. In her spare time, she enjoys reading, traveling, cooking, swimming, and playing tennis.

Made in the USA
Monee, IL
08 May 2023

33299024R00138